Loving Your
Parents
When They Can
No Longer Love You

TERRY D. HARGRAVE

Loving Your
Parents
When They Can
No Longer Love You

ZONDERVAN™

GRAND RAPIDS, MICHIGAN 49530 USA

ZONDERVAN™

Loving Your Parents When They Can No Longer Love You
Copyright © 2005 by Terry Hargrave

Requests for information should be addressed to:
Zondervan, *Grand Rapids, Michigan 49530*

Library of Congress Cataloging-in-Publication Data

Hargrave, Terry D.
    Loving your parents when they can no longer love you / Terry D. Hargrave.
      p. cm.
   ISBN-10: 0-310-25563-5 (softcover)
   ISBN-13: 978-0-310-25563-5 (softcover)
  1. Aging parents—Care. 2. Aging parents—Care—Religious aspects—
Christianity. 3. Frail elderly—Home care. 4. Adult children of aging parents—
Family relationships. 5. Caregivers—Psychology. I. Title.
   HQ1063.6.H37 2004
   306.874—dc22

                2004023478

Interior design by Beth Shagene

Printed in the United States of America

05 06 07 08 09 10 11 12 /❖ DCI/ 10 9 8 7 6 5 4 3 2

For Genevieve

Contents

Part 3: Embracing the Hope of Defeat

Introduction

This is a book about struggle. It is the struggle to be weak when we desire to be strong, to be helpless when we want power, and to be sacrificial when we'd really rather be selfish. This is a book about struggle.

It is not a struggle that exists so much between the generations of caregiver and older person but rather one between all people and life. Aging, in this generation and at this time in history, just happens to be the vehicle through which the struggle seems most evident and present.

On the one hand, we desire to control our destinies, implement our wills, and enjoy the freedom to choose when, how, and who we love and who will love us. Western society bombards us with these desires. We want to decide our career paths and educational backgrounds, achieve financial security and neighborhood safety, and have convenient and close relationships. Most of the time we can ignore situations where our needed talents receive little compensation. We can remain ignorant of the needs of the world and so use our financial resources for our own desires. And we can cocoon ourselves tightly in predictable and emotionally neutral relationships.

But then there's the other hand. God wants us to understand the value of vulnerability, weakness, and sacrifice—and it is in these vulnerable states that God's power becomes active in our lives. As Paul says in 2 Corinthians 12:10, it is in our weakness that God makes us strong. Most of us know this fact and feel more than willing to cooperate—at least, until weakness really touches our lives. The struggle for us comes down to becoming the weak ambassadors of a mighty God, in the face of our desire to exercise control, power, and choice.

Enter aging. Precisely at this time in history when we seem to have so much ability to control information and so many reasons to get self-focused, our parents and family are living longer than at any period in modern history. Medicine has devised ways to keep people alive, but a good percentage of them will have chronic health problems that demand care from others. Who will provide this care? If you are reading this book, chances are you are currently a caregiver or see caregiving in your near future. In caregiving we lose a good part of the control of our lives, we become powerless to determine outcomes, and we must put our needs behind theirs. Aging and caregiving in the twenty-first century force us to struggle with the reality of life. This book is about how we work within this struggle but also how we are changed by the struggle.

Aging, of course, is not optional. It is like a giant vacuum cleaner that will eventually suck us all up. You can pour on the lotions to smooth out the wrinkles and mix in the dye to color the hair, but you will not be able to cover up the problems and challenges that aging presents to the family.

Perhaps the biggest problem of all occurs when we confront the complex reality of giving care to an older parent. When you consider your busy schedule, how deeply you long to control your own life, and how frail and needy your parents have become, the job of caregiving can stress the living daylights out of you.

Loving Your Parents When They Can No Longer Love You comes out of personal experience. I have cared for older people in a personal care facility, and my wife and I have cared for my mother-in-law, who has Alzheimer's disease. This book will bring you face-to-face with some of the hard-hitting realities that must be faced, such as taking care of your parent's legal and financial issues, choosing where to live, the type of care your parent will need, and how to deal with physical and emotional health problems. Much of what I suggest comes from my years of studying aging families as a professor and therapist, but most everything in this book has been worked out in the school of hard knocks in my own experiences of caregiving.

This is not just another book about how to care for aging parents, however, or even how to care for yourself while you provide the care. It is at its core a book on how you can lovingly and tenderly embrace the job of caregiving as a spiritual journey that can deepen your faith while strengthening your character.

Caregiving is both a story and a journey. I intend for this book to help you grasp the importance and opportunity of the job you have taken (or are about to take) and to assist you in creating your own special story and journey—and what a journey it can be! A journey to the depths of learning how selfish and withholding we can be, to the difficulty of managing the day-to-day work of care, to the desperation of learning how to hold on to God when no more hope or energy remains. I hope yours will be a journey and story like mine, one that has changed me in ways from which I wish never to recover.

PART 1

Embracing Caregiving and Aging as a Spiritual Journey

Consider it pure joy, my brothers, whenever you face trials of many kinds, because you know that the testing of your faith develops perseverance. Perseverance must finish its work so that you may be mature and complete, not lacking anything.

James 1:2–4

Congratulations! You have been elected. Maybe you slid into the job a little at a time; perhaps it happened with a single phone call. But if you are reading this book, chances are you are, or very soon will become, the caregiver for your older parent. It is a big job, and at one time or another, it will take you to the very edge of your physical and emotional strength.

What's in it for you? All sorts of good things, like brokenness and humility. Consider caregiving a spiritual obstacle course—it'll do you good, but it'll also present you with a series of potent challenges.

While we tend to equate comfort with joy, the biblical writer James talks about a different kind of joy: the knowledge that we are being made into spiritual people, people who at the end of life will lack nothing. God means for life to mold us into a spiritual condition fit for the kingdom of heaven. It is not our prerogative, nor is it in our control, to fit the spiritual life around the pleasures of this earthly life. For those of us who live with the obligations of caregiving, nothing is more difficult than to grasp this concept. Yet nothing is more precious.

1

In Two Years
She Will Be Dependent

That is why, for Christ's sake, I delight in weaknesses,
in insults, in hardships, in persecutions, in difficulties.
For when I am weak, then I am strong.
2 Corinthians 12:10

While some people hold the aging in high regard, most in our society treat them with contempt. Consider the knowing jokes and so-called wisdom about aging in our culture:

- Growing old isn't so bad; it certainly beats the alternative.
- I'm not eighty-one years old, I'm eighty-one years *young*.
- Growing old is not for sissies!

Attitudes and beliefs about aging vary about as much as there are people in the world. Most of us, however, have at least some attitude of defiance toward aging. We work against the natural flow of physical deterioration with Botox injections, antiaging potions and pills, and fashions that disguise and cosmetic surgeries that mislead.

And yet, aging comes nonetheless.

15

THE FRIGHT OF AGING

My first experience with aging scared me. As a young boy, I sat in a small tar-paper house that, as a man, I could cross in four strides. Its turn-of-the-century gaslights made a constant coughing sound, as though your head were caught in a waterfall. A potbelly stove supposedly warmed the meager abode, but poor ventilation made the task almost impossible. I did not breathe the thick, musty air as much as I had to swallow it.

The house belonged to my father's father, a man I would come to respect and love. This orchard farmer from southwest Colorado had experienced a hard life with his wife and twelve children. He had only one arm, having lost the other in a railroad accident during the Great Depression.

As I sat on the stoop of one room, he tried to coax me out of my shyness into conversing and playing with him. "Come here and let me hold you," he would say. He didn't know it was not shyness but terror that kept me in the shadows. His aging face, scraggly beard, and one arm unnerved me. It seemed to my young eyes he had come straight out of the horror shows that delighted my brothers and me. He looked so *unnatural*. My small mind could not imagine anyone could ever end up in such shape. He looked and spoke spooky.

So I made up my mind as a five-year-old to avoid older people. At times I couldn't avoid them—around Thanksgiving or Christmas, for example—but as a whole, I could look the other way and never feel concerned about their lives. Most of all, I could remain safe from all that fear.

But at one point in my life I finally decided to look the issue in the eye. I was in graduate school when I learned that my mother's father lay dying of stomach cancer. He had written me off when I was a kid. He didn't believe I had worked as hard on his ranch as my older brothers had. He never called me by my proper name and failed to attend my wedding. We had an issue between us, to put it mildly. But because he was my grandfather and I felt obligated to see him before he died, I traveled with my wife and mother to see him one last time.

The weekend passed with little to note, but when the time came to say a final good-bye, I felt lost and disoriented. I had no words with which to bid him farewell. I had nothing honest to say to him. So I let him pass me by, like a stranger with whom I had brushed sleeves on the street. I did not feel that I "blew my opportunity," like dropping a last-second pass that could have won the football game; it was more like I'd never even stepped on the field. To this day, I can remember my total lack of effort. It shames me still.

"I will never let a moment like that pass by again without at least trying to make connection," I later said to my wife. As a budding family therapist, I knew that families everywhere struggled with these issues. I felt a missionary zeal to help these families avoid the despair and shame I felt. As a result, I took a position as a personal care facility director with a visionary friend of mine who was committed to create progressive older communities. I had energy and zeal but didn't know much about the process of aging. I did lots of reading, but my most valuable teacher became the older people themselves.

The very first older person I met from the facility was a retired accountant named Dixon. Mucus drained from his hook nose, rolling down in beads on the oxygen tubes attached to his nostrils. His emphysema and respiratory problems surely resulted from long years of smoking. Burn marks dotted his furniture, and he reeked of greasy hair and stale body odor. And he was *mean*. No one visited him, and we all assumed he had verbally abused his family into a permanent cutoff. He yelled at my staff, and he yelled at me, as if to proclaim that his life was justified and the rest of us were idiots. He would rant, "I haven't lived this long to have to put up with you kind of people!" He was, in many ways, the living rule book on how to age without grace.

This time I did not feel fear, although all his maladies did cause me some discomfort. This time I felt embarrassment—embarrassment to see a human being who had progressed to such a sad shape he could no longer take care of basic body functions or govern his angry emotions. He didn't seem to mind the stuff dripping from his nose or care what anyone else thought of him. Dixon was a man out of control, an extremely weak man who still thought of himself as powerful. How pathetic to see someone in that condition and in that kind of quandary! I wanted him to cover himself with guile or pretense in order to make the whole aging thing look better than it actually did. At the same time, I felt welling up within me my old tendency to run away. I wanted to withdraw—but this time I stayed.

Ever since, despite the fear and embarrassment, I have been willing to look straight-eyed and full-faced into aging.

WHAT IS AGING?

What is this thing called aging? First and foremost, it is a process of maturity as natural as taking one's first step. Yet a special twist to aging makes it particularly difficult. These steps we take are heading us toward our own demise.

Let me be clear. I do not believe that aging is one long, depressing death march in which we inevitably do less and less and wander more and more. We can be productive and vital well into our sixties, seventies, eighties, and some of us, into our nineties. No chronology magically states when we are old enough to be identified as the "aging population." Some people are old before they get out of their fifties; others are still going strong long after most people their age have died. We can remain vital for a long time.

In many ways, this is what we all desire—to be vital and alive for a good long time and then die in our sleep. We love to hear the stories of the ninety-one-year-old woman who plays jazz piano in a club, or the eighty-six-year-old man who completes a marathon. But these stories aren't really about aging and don't well represent the aging process.

For the purposes of this book, when I speak about aging, I mean that time of life when disease or wear has taken a toll big enough to significantly diminish or remove entirely one's ability to function in an independent manner. This is particularly important to the family, because, by my definition, an old person needs care.

This "being old" flies in the face of what most in the Western world say they want out of life. Old means, at the minimum, that we no longer get to hold on to our lives. It means the aging process has advanced to such a point that we can no longer pretend our physical lives will go on forever. It means we are nearing death. We cannot hold on to our health, our wealth, our precious belongings, or even our essential relationships. At first blush, being old is not the opposite of young but the opposite of *life*. Can anyone in the modern age actually look at this process and not be afraid and embarrassed and want to turn and run away?

I believe we can. In fact, I believe it's a must for anyone who calls himself or herself a Christian. And if we willingly look at the process of aging and being old, we will find the essential elements of discipleship and the kingdom of God.

Who needs the process of aging? We do.

THE COURAGE OF FAITH, THE HUMILITY OF LOVE

We need aging because it is quickly becoming a defining and sanctifying process in the lives of Christians. Whether we are the older person or the caregiver of an older person, the aging process forces us to recognize that we do not control our own lives, that we have little say in how the future will progress, and that any fruitful effort is born out of humility.

Of course, these ideas probably sound familiar, because the Bible is chock-full of just such commands on what it takes to become a man or a woman of God. Remember the words of our faith—words we say we believe?

> Do nothing out of selfish ambition or vain conceit, but in humility consider others better than yourselves. Each of you should look not only to your own interests, but also to the interests of others.
> Your attitude should be the same as that of Christ Jesus.
>
> Philippians 2:3–5

Such a simple phrase—our attitudes should be the same as that of Jesus. We commit to God, by faith, to remain his through the thick and thin of life. We bind ourselves to God in the same way the smith uses heat and strength to forge metal to metal.

But God is also committed to us. He's committed to making us into the image and attitude of Christ Jesus. And what is that attitude?

> Who, being in very nature God,
>   did not consider equality with God something
>   to be grasped,
> but made himself nothing,
>   taking the very nature of a servant,
>   being made in human likeness.
> And being found in appearance as a man,
>   he humbled himself
>   and became obedient to death—
>   even death on a cross!
>
> Philippians 2:6–8

Very simply, God is committed to us becoming humble servants. This is the way of the cross, the way of Jesus, and the way all of us are to follow.

When a person in our family becomes old and requires care, what we have only thought about suddenly becomes an emotional reality. The sacrifice we make as a caregiver for an elderly person requires strong character and the attitude of Christ, and it's a very different thing from giving care to a child. The child grows, becomes stronger, and interacts more and more. Our sacrifice for our children no doubt teaches us much, but it focuses on a young man or woman who is built for the future. It is a hopeful humility. When we give care to an older person, however, we sacrifice for one who grows weaker, interacts less, and eventually will die. It is a service and sacrifice for which we see very little—maybe even nothing. Caregiving for an older person is purely about servanthood.

Surely, this kind of sacrificial giving is exactly what Jesus Christ exercised in his great love for us. At this time in history, God has created an opportunity for us to learn what it really means to love one another. Caregiving means accepting the humble place of servanthood. And the opportunity exists right in our own families!

God molds us into Christlikeness through our own aging processes. The older person in need of care must recognize that life is coming to an end. There is no room for self-sufficiency and defiance. Being old—really old—means finding the precarious balance between doing what we can and relying on others to fill in the gaps. This process of letting go and entrusting ourselves to others demands a kind of courage made possible only by faith.

Many older people in our society chant the mantra, "I don't want to become a burden to my children." While this expression is well-meant, it is, sadly, misguided.

When we speak such a phrase, most often we are really saying we never want to turn over control of ourselves to someone else. We certainly don't want them to have to serve us! It is a step of tremendous faith to embrace the idea that God uses our growing old and our caregiving to mold us into humble and courageous servants.

This kind of faith is born of struggle because growing old, as well as accepting and providing care, is anything but easy. Not everyone will have to experience the full process, but for those who do and thus are being trained by the great aging task, it will bring forth the courage of faith and the humility of love.

Caregiver and older person are not called to avoid burdens for one another; we are called to lay them aside for the greater burden of Christ.

> Come to me, all you who are weary and burdened, and I will give you rest. Take my yoke upon you and learn from me, for I am gentle and humble in heart, and you will find rest for your souls. For my yoke is easy and my burden is light.
>
> Matthew 11:28–30

If we are able to embrace growing old and caregiving as the yoke of Christ, we will not try to minimize the impact the process has on our lives. Instead, we will recognize that this precious yoke that requires us to be humble and courageous is meant to yield a unique gift—the gift of rest and peace. It is not an easy gift, but for those who are willing to take it on, it will bring peace.

HEROIC TO HUMBLE

Caregivers and older people are not locked in a battle against each other. We are in a dance, a dance that requires a balance of intimacy of communication, humility of yielding to one another, and courage to trust the process. We do not have to do the dance perfectly; we just have to keep moving. If we keep dancing, God will use our faithfulness to produce the valuable fruits of peace, joy, and love.

In my own life, I did not immediately recognize how this process built the amazing character and attitude of Christ within me. But as I kept moving to the rhythm of aging, I found out more about myself than at any other time in my life. And the way of Christ became alive to me.

When I first began working at the personal care facility with some eighty residents, I truly believed in what I was doing. I wanted to learn from, minister to, and care for elderly people and their families. I also felt compelled to work on issues within my own family to resolve old wounds so we could communicate and love better.

I felt I was "doing good" among people who needed me. I felt like the Lone Ranger, who rode in heroically to help people out of seemingly impossible messes. As I worked my way through graduate school, I studied elderly people and their families in clinical settings. I tried new techniques to help older people to function better and families to express love and care in constructive ways. By the time I neared the end of my graduate work, I felt I knew all about aging. I knew the important things about the process. I knew what to look for, how to be effective, and how to help the elderly person and his or her family finish well. I had worked with many older persons in a caregiving role, but none more closely than my mother-in-law, Genevieve.

And only then did I realize how little I knew.

A WORTHY AND COURAGEOUS WOMAN WITH A PROBLEM

Genevieve was a remarkable woman in so many ways. Although the top of her head reached only to the middle of my chest, her courage and steadfastness always left a deep impression on me. Even as a fourteen-year-old, when I met her daughter in junior high school, I knew our whole community sympathized with her and held her in high regard. This woman knew how to persevere through searing pain and still make life positive.

As a young adult, this youngest of three children from an Oklahoma family married Bill, a Harvard Business School graduate who had become a southern California advertising executive. Bill and Genevieve had four beautiful children together, three boys and a girl who would one day become my wife. Bill, a fun and gregarious man, always seemed a little bigger than life. He and Genevieve knew some of the famous and beautiful people of Hollywood, and they were beautiful people themselves. He had his boys out on the tennis courts at the club before they reached the age of five and always seemed eager for the next adventure. He was older and more confident than Genevieve, and he was very successful. But he also struggled with clinical depression. When business setbacks in 1960 hounded him during one of those bouts, he made the unfortunate decision to take his own life.

Everything Genevieve knew—home, housekeeping, mothering—got ripped to shreds in the hurricane of her husband's suicide. Imagine how this woman, at the age of thirty-five, must have felt as she faced life with four young children to raise. She made the courageous decision to move her young family from southern California to Amarillo, Texas, to live in a small town closer to her brother. After living in Amarillo for a year, her life began to stabilize. She joined a Presbyterian church and moved into a stable neighborhood, and her brother consistently provided a positive male presence in her family.

One day, however, her oldest son, Bruce, came home ill. Over the next couple of weeks he got steadily sicker, and one Friday evening Genevieve hastily summoned her brother and an ambulance. Before the night ended, Bruce had died from acute leukemia.

Somehow Genevieve gathered herself, and with grit and determination she continued to raise her children in a healthy and positive environment. She pieced together her life around making them a success. Her two remaining sons, David and John, got good grades in school and became skilled tennis players. Sharon, my future wife, loved horses and excelled at equestrian activities with her own horses, Macaroni and Geronimo. Genevieve made life "normal" for these kids in the face of tragedy that would have crippled most of us. When most of us would have crawled into a foxhole, this gifted, strong, and sacrificial woman led the charge and set up supply lines to her children. She was remarkable.

But she was far from perfect. Agonizing thoughts and memories haunted her, and she began to drink to numb her raw emotions and soothe her pain. As David and John grew, occasionally they'd see Genevieve's drinking get out of control and impair her judgment. David, the oldest, would reassure Sharon, "It's just a small thing she has to do to keep going." It's not hard to understand his perspective. Who can say that we, too, might not turn to drinking if we were to lose both a spouse and a child? The drinking didn't appear to interfere much with the rhythms of an otherwise happy family.

In 1970, however, the walls came crashing in once again. David, a natural leader and a great friend to many people, shared his father's appetite for laughter and adventure. David was attending Oklahoma University at the time, and one evening a pathological killer ambushed him and his date. The man locked them in a car trunk and murdered them in a grisly fashion more suited to a battlefield than to a college campus.

Genevieve's family of six had now been reduced to three. Some wounded families lose half of their members, but seldom do they lose them one at a time in such painful and shocking ways. My future wife and brother-in-law felt over-whelmed. But somehow, Genevieve managed to gather herself once more and reassure her children, "It will be OK. We will be OK." Despite the pain, she resolved to move her family forward.

Both John and Sharon graduated from high school and col-lege, got married, and by the mid-1980s began to start families of their own. With the addition of spouses and grandchildren, it really began to feel as if it *was* OK. Maybe, just maybe, all of us really *were* OK.

Aging: Who Needs It?

In 1989, the University of Mississippi offered me a position to teach marriage and family classes to undergraduate students. It was a dream come true. I loved education and had always fantasized about teaching at the university level.

My wife and I settled in with our one-year-old daughter. My wife's brother, John, and his wife had started their family in Michigan. Our jobs felt secure. We took vacations together. Genevieve would travel to Mississippi and to Michigan for long visits. It was a solid time of having so much fun together, watching our families grow and become close.

Just two years later, the wheels began to come off. Almost a quarter of a century after the fact, a district attorney decided to prosecute someone for the murder of Genevieve's son and his friend. Although there always had been suspicions that a certain police officer had committed the awful crime, no charges were ever filed. We had learned to live with the real-ity that we'd never know the circumstances surrounding David's death. The new investigation felt like shears cutting through the fabric of peaceful family life.

Fears unfelt in years suddenly began to torment my wife, Sharon. "Keep the curtains closed," she instructed. "I just don't

know if that crazy person who killed David is out there somewhere." Thoughts of long-denied justice came into John's mind
as it began to look more likely that the district attorney would
pursue prosecution. And then there was Genevieve. Genevieve
simply seemed lost. Snagged once again in a tragedy out of the
past, this time with no family around to tend to her pain, her
drinking increased.

When charges were finally filed against a suspect, the district attorney's office went on something of a witch hunt to
scare up evidence. Since most of the evidence from the case
had somehow mysteriously disappeared, the DA tried to find
circumstantial evidence. The sordid story ran in newspapers
and on popular tabloid television shows. All of this was agonizing and traumatized everyone in the family.

Sharon, John, and Genevieve got thrown back in time,
landing in a foxhole in the midst of a raging battle. I was in the
battle also but in a different foxhole. I could only watch as my
family relived its days of pain. I could do nothing but try to be
available. Most of all, I felt I needed to be more available to
Genevieve. Just before the trial, I took a job at a community
college and moved back to Amarillo, Texas, so we could live
in the same area as Genevieve.

I knew it was the right thing to do. I really didn't know how
it would work out, but I had a strong conviction that if Sharon,
my children, and I were in the same town as Genevieve, somehow we could provide a shield to deflect some of her misery.
I could help put an end to the tearing of the fabric of our family. But my choice meant leaving a place I loved, taking a job
that felt like a step down to me, and moving to a place to
which I had no desire to return.

We made the move, but it did not stop the pain. The trial
featured two weeks of gory details about the murder and things
we would have preferred not to know. Two weeks of the prosecution wandering through weak circumstantial evidence,

aware that the real evidence had never been found. Two weeks that ended in a "not guilty" verdict.

We tried to hold each other close, but Genevieve never quite recovered. Her sorrow spiraled into out-of-control drinking. She couldn't stand to see her grandchildren take even the smallest risk, from swinging at the park to walking in the mud. Her anxiety, sadness, and alcoholism isolated her more and more until her social world had shrunk down essentially to us.

And I was stuck in Amarillo. I had reasoned that my heroic sacrifice to take care of my mother-in-law would last a year or two, and then I'd move back to a university position. I longed for the research and vitality of university life. The landscape in Amarillo felt barren and depressing to me.

Primarily, however, my effort to heal my family and take care of Genevieve had ended in utter failure. She continued to go downhill. I felt desperate for escape. I would apply for jobs and get close to getting an offer but always seemed to end up the second or third choice. The move from university to community college created questions about whether I could write, do research, or reach tenure. After four years, I remained mired in a job I hated, in a place I loathed, taking care of a woman who could not be cared for.

As I saw it, all my heroic efforts had ended in a hopeless failure. As Genevieve started slipping into dementia and losing control, I slipped into a clinical depression. I had always tied my self-worth to my success in my job, family, and relationships. Yet now my career seemed frozen, my family had fractured, and in my anger and bitterness, I found myself withdrawing from relationships. I remember saying to several of my friends, "I feel like I used to be a rookie pitcher who won games in the World Series, and now I'm playing for a local farm club."

But God was at work in my life. He wasn't trying to make me a heroic man of God or a mighty warrior for Christ; he was trying to make me a humble servant with the attitude of Jesus. Slowly I began to realize the folly of tying my personal worth to my job. I started to conclude that I would serve wherever I was and that I would be thankful for the life and relationships I had. The depression eventually lifted—but still I felt immobilized and frustrated because of Genevieve's continued decline. Her life became so narrow that my children and I got squeezed out. She no longer dropped by our house and seldom invited us to hers. I could see her memory slipping and her unexplained anxiety increasing, along with an inability to manage her drinking and personal affairs.

It was time to step in. John and his wife and Sharon and I sat around our dining room table seven years ago to set out a plan to confront Genevieve's alcoholism and to plan for her eventual care. I knew all about the process of aging. I let everyone know I suspected that Genevieve had Alzheimer's disease and boldly predicted, "In two years, she will be dependent." Sadly, I was correct.

We sought help and made several efforts to intervene yet again to address the alcoholism, to little effect. As Genevieve continued to withdraw, her life continued to unravel. Within two years she became ill and had a minor stroke, which prompted us to take a direct role in her caregiving. We moved her first to a retirement facility that provided meals, then to a personal care home that provided more supervision. More recently we transferred her to an Alzheimer's facility.

Over the course of five years, we had to slowly take over responsibility for her medication regime, her financial decisions, her bathing and hygiene, and her plan for health care. All this we did in a willing manner because we saw it as our responsibility. Although I felt that God was working in my life and breaking my self-focus, I still tried to take care of Genevieve out of my own "heroic" strength. I thought of myself as a good son-in-law. I thought I was living out what I had taught so many people about aging.

I was mistaken.

My world crashed during the summer of 2000. Genevieve was living at a retirement facility that provided meals when I received a call from the cook. "There's something really wrong with Genevieve," she said. "She's unable to stand by herself and doesn't make sense." She appeared to be paralyzed on the right side of her body, her speech was slurred and incoherent, and she was on the edge of consciousness. Because I knew the process of aging, I would have bet the farm she had suffered another stroke. I made arrangements to get her to the hospital, called Sharon, and got in touch with Genevieve's neurologist—who also guessed it was a stroke.

While technicians drew blood at the hospital, performed tests, and prepared for an MRI, Sharon and I discussed options for future care and what the stroke would mean for our lives. As we held Genevieve's hand and reassured one another, the neurologist came into the room with a sheepish grin on her face. She showed us the test results and said, "Her blood alcohol level is high. She's drunk."

I don't recall the exact order of things after these words floated around the room and finally lodged into my consciousness, but I do remember feeling overcome by anger. I do remember the furious words spewing out of my mouth. "You are so selfish!" I raged. "You think the only thing we have to do is take care of you! Don't you realize how you're ruining my life?"

After Genevieve began sobering up, I took her to the car to return her to her apartment, my vicious words echoing in my head. Genevieve apologized, but I knew all of my heroic efforts through the years had been wasted. Within a few hours, I reached a surprising conclusion: the failure didn't rest with Genevieve alone but also with me. Here was a woman who had suffered great pain, yet with phenomenal dignity. She had given herself unselfishly to her children and provided a normal and supportive life for them when she had had every excuse to shut down. She had dedicated herself to nothing else but trying to keep her lineage healthy and secure. And here I was, angrily shouting accusations of selfishness and blame.

That's when I knew who I really was. I had always thought of myself as a good man, a man who would give of himself to help others. I had been willing to go the extra mile to make somebody else's life better. I had performed well as a heroic and sacrificial person; I had put my career behind the needs of my family.

All of these things were partially true—as long as my career got back on track, as long as people recognized my "extraordinary" work, and as long as Genevieve responded cooperatively and graciously. But after I heard myself shouting at my dear mother-in-law, I saw a large part of me that was harsh, unloving, demanding, and angry. It first took a clinical depression and then Genevieve to finally get the point across to me. I was a man who demanded the power to make things happen so they'd meet my goals, the need to control my own destiny, and the freedom to have things my way. I knew God had brought me to a confrontation with my own character, a confrontation that would result in my either pretending to be a hero or truly embracing the role of humble servant and caregiver.

WHEN LOVE IS DIFFICULT

The issue of Genevieve's alcoholism has long faded, since she no longer has access to the drug. But my experience with her helped me realize how difficult it is to love someone who cannot or does not respond. I began to see that it's often the very people who need to be loved and cared for the most who will not or cannot accept it. I now see that love does not have to see response, nor does it have to understand. Love simply loves. As James tells us, "Religion that God our Father accepts as pure and faultless is this: to look after orphans and widows in their distress" (James 1:27).

The royal law means caring for those who are unlovable, just as we wish to be loved. Only this kind of love demonstrates the kind of agape, altruistic love that is essential. It is this type of love that God demonstrated for us in Jesus Christ.

Most of us greatly misunderstand what agape love is all about. Humanistic psychology in the last half of the twentieth century began to equate agape love with something called "unconditional love," or "unconditional positive regard." We began to think of agape as love that accepted the beloved, no matter what.

But while agape no doubt has this aspect of "acceptance," it is not the prime element. Instead, the prime element is self-sacrifice. Agape gives, not out of abundance with plenty left over, but in a way that may leave it with little or nothing.

One morsel of bread—I need it for sustenance, or I will die; you also need it to survive. Both of us stand on the edge of starvation. But agape causes me to look at you and say, "Take it and eat." I say this, knowing it means my demise. But I say it because I agape you.

Once I started to understand this, I no longer wanted to be a heroic man. Now I want to be a humble man who loves simply because this is what Christ does for me. It took me more than a decade to get that message, and it required leaving a position I loved; taking a job I hated; leaving a beautiful, forested land for a flat, ugly prairie; and saying good-bye to the accolades of professional colleagues in order to provide frustrating care to a needy and usually unresponsive old woman.

But the exchange has yielded pure gold. The precious gift of the greatest lesson of my life is how to love as Christ loves me.

EMBRACING THE AGING PROCESS

le of caregiving. But I s the yoke Christ has can stand the test of

mbrace. They provide ut as I have traversed iritual journey and my

ity, no matter the tem- ny relationship with e.

a Who, Dr. Seuss tells in the coolness of a d going about his day s. He hears, ever so speck of dust floating there must be a small culture, at stake. So civilization—at great ly one who can hear

ss to take care of. Yet Ve are here." We can will take up the chal- he only way we can

costs us dearly. Our ur financial picture ns may be hindered. erson who depends

y indeed, it is our entire civilization. it is in the very small cries for help that we find the measure of who we are—how we respond to the very least of these our brothers and sisters (see Matthew 25:40).

Self-sacrifice lies at the heart of a healthy civilization. It dawns on us that when we sacrifice ourselves for the good of the whole—or even the one—we work toward the greater good of humanity.

When we hear the soft whispers of our elders, crying for help, we may well be the only ones who will hear. But if we respond, we will be changed. And in providing care for our elderly companions, we will also be providing care for our own souls. We will not only strengthen and build our character, we will also strengthen our civilization. Sacrifice and humility—this is what caregiving is all about.

THE STRUGGLE CONTINUES

Yes, this is a story of struggle. It is the struggle to be weak when we desire to be strong, helpless when we want power, and sacrificial when we are selfish. But in the story of struggle, we gain the greatest gifts in life. We receive gifts that mold and shape our characters, gifts with the power not only to change our relationships but the relationships of our children's children's children as well.

Do I love Genevieve perfectly? Certainly not. I've only just begun to learn about humility and the power that love has to change my heart. My heart does not change because she loves me; it changes because I love her. The gift of weakness, humility, and sacrifice is the gold we must seek.

Aging is life. If you have the courage to embrace it and to see what it can teach you, then let us share this time in the telling of our stories.

QUESTIONS FOR CONSIDERATION

1. What things do you hate about the aging process and your role as a caregiver?

2. Do some of the things you hate point to character flaws in you? If so, do they have the potential to help you grow?

3. How can you step over the flaw and head toward the redemptive part of aging that gives life?

It Is Never Too Late
to Finish Family Business

Instead, everyone will die for his own sin; whoever
eats sour grapes—his own teeth will be set on edge.
Jeremiah 31:30

In many ways, family life and development is like a great drama
played out on the stage of community. We grow into adulthood
and find ourselves center stage at the height of our financial
earning power, impact on others, and influence on our nuclear
families. Many of us will have a spouse and children who sur-
round us, and all will focus on what we do and how we are.

But as our children grow into adulthood and start having
families of their own, we begin to find ourselves pushed away
from center stage. While we'll continue to have strong supporting roles to the main actors, the action of life's drama
clearly is orchestrated by the younger generations of our adult
children and grandchildren. And as the decades pass, our
grandchildren begin to take the center stage for their own solil-
oquies. Our middle-aged children are cast into their supporting acting roles—and we find ourselves on the edge of the
stage, barely part of the large chorus. And when our time
comes, we slip behind the curtain and make our final exit from
the family.

If we play our parts well, our family audience will appreciate us, and we'll feel a great sense of accomplishment and satisfaction. Our relatives will applaud us—as at a skillfully executed performance—and our examples will serve as good models of wisdom for years to come. Our seamless transitions and our skill in productive living will make everyone else in our family play their parts better. I've seen people live their lives in exactly this manner, and it is such a beautiful and satisfying thing when they pass from this life to the next. At their funerals, amidst the sadness and mourning, sweet memories and thankfulness abound for such lives.

But others do not play their parts so well. They take center stage and use the time to focus exclusively on themselves. Like scene-stealers who demand the spotlight, they refuse to cooperate with anyone else in the family. Even when it is their time to move to the supporting roles or the chorus, they tenaciously hold on to the limelight, to everyone's dismay. Not only do their performances go unappreciated, they throw off the whole family's acting rhythm, resulting in a massive flop. I've also seen many of these people at the end of life. They do exit the stage, yet it's often kicking and screaming. But instead of seeing a family that has appreciated the performance, I see an open wound of pain. In place of sweet memories, I hear a collective sigh of, "Whew! I'm glad that's over." It is a pain that grief cannot resolve.

For those who have aging cast members who fit this model of bad actors in a family production, caregiving presents special challenges and questions:

- How do I handle my anger and hurt when I have to change, bathe, or feed this old man? He never lifted a finger to do anything for me!
- She has manipulated and taken advantage of me all my life. Must I still put up with it now?

- He has been selfish all his life. I don't see why it should be my responsibility to pay one cent toward his care.

You can imagine how gut-wrenching the experience can be. Imagine your worst relative, whom you are obligated to see over the holidays. Now, multiply this feeling by ten, and then saddle up for the interaction 365 days a year. Caring for someone who has behaved badly for years is like living around an open grave. It stinks.

WHY ARE WE OBLIGATED?

Herb was a thin, raggedy man who lived on the second floor of the personal care facility I directed. When he walked, his joints seemed to be barely holding together; he looked like a button ready to drop off a coat. He divorced when his children were young, retired from his job as a middle manager of an oil company, and despised life. He mostly stayed to himself.

So Herb might have slipped off the radar screen without much notice had it not been for one thing. He had a brain tumor and was becoming more incapacitated, thus needing some care from his children. I met with Herb to discuss a plan for his care.

"I have three kids—a girl and two boys. I don't think they'll want much to do with me now," he said sheepishly.

He was right. When I contacted the oldest daughter, Julie, she stated flatly, "He can die alone for all I care!" The two sons, Bill and Bob, seemed a bit more conciliatory, but they made it clear they did not like or approve of Herb. The youngest son, Bob, told me, "He was always putting us down at home. He was mostly uninterested in us when we were young and simply left us alone when our mother divorced him. He always acted like we owed him something. To tell you the truth, he deserves what he's getting. I don't see why we should be obligated to care for him at all."

Family damage reminds me of the big bang theory. Scientists had hypothesized about a big bang for years, but once they pointed their radio telescopes toward the heavens, they began recording all sorts of background radiation noise—noise associated with the creation of the universe. It's as though the universe is still speaking, the waves created by the original explosion still reverberating all around us in a cacophony of primordial history. Family damage is much like that. It happened in the past, but the noise of the event very much reverberates around us in the present. It is very real and governs the emotional temperature of family relationships.

Good Christian caregivers have to struggle hard with the reality of providing care for irresponsible and damaging parents. It's not as though we can forget Jesus' commands to turn the other cheek (Matthew 5:39) and to forgive as we wish to be forgiven (Matthew 18:21–35); it's simply that the toxins from those relationships are much more potent than those from other relationships. It's not like feeling angry with a business partner who cheated you or feeling hurt because of a friend who spread a vicious rumor. Old family memories of indignations or shame or devastation overwhelm us, like a nasty virus that incapacitates a computer's hard drive. It feels awful—worse than other indignities, because, in fact, it *is* worse.

Why? The parent-child relationship is like no other. When a parent brings a child into the world, the child is completely helpless and has no other resource but the parent to provide nurture. Indeed, the parent is *responsible* and *obligated* to provide such care. And it's not merely the feeding, sheltering, and changing of diapers that is important. A parent is responsible for sculpting the basic belief system of the newborn, including his or her self-image and style of relating. This is the original programming task, and it is unique to the parent-child bond.

This program gets inputted into the soul of a child essentially through the elements of *love* and *trust*. How a parent loves a child teaches that child about who the child is. If I treat my children like they are precious prizes, worthy of my sacrifice and desirable enough that I will want to be with them, then they will likely grow up believing they are precious, worthy, and not alone. If I give to them freely of my time and resources and teach them to give of theirs, they likely will learn that relationships can be safe and trustworthy. We learn who we are and how to relate in the world through the essential elements of love and trust. These basic beliefs are forged most easily and solidly when we are babies. It is not merely the parent's *job* to serve as the blacksmith in the child's formation; it is his or her *obligation*.

Most of us have parents who adequately assured us that we were loved and that our families were safe and their relationships trustworthy. In such cases, we typically have only the "normal" relationship issues and thus face caregiving for our parents with few, if any, unusual emotional concerns.

But some of us came from families where love and trustworthiness either got portioned out in meager increments as from an eyedropper or seemed absent altogether. In these cases, either one or both of the parents reneged on their obligation and defaulted on the most essential elements of parenting. Perhaps they were alcoholic, selfish, manipulative, abusive, neglectful, passive, or a hundred other possibilities—but whatever they were, they left us on the short end of feeling emotionally fulfilled and physically secure. In short, they cheated us out of what a dependent infant and child is entitled to receive. We grew up in an atmosphere where one or both parents acted irresponsibly, and it was unfair.

And we did not forget. When such irresponsible parents come to need *our* care, bullets of emotional resentment start ricocheting off every part of our minds. It's as though our hearts say, "How dare you ask for care now! How can you ask me to do for you what you refused to do when I was in need?" Of course, our hearts have a legitimate claim, just as Julie and Bob declared about their father, Herb: "He deserves to die alone, and I am not obligated to help him in any way."

When I offered to meet with Julie, Bill, and Bob to try to settle some issues concerning Herb and his care, they all showed up. A few adult children simply refuse to have *anything* to do with their older parent in need, but most are like Julie, Bill, and Bob. Despite their deep resentments and hurt, they also desire some sense of peace. Regardless of what we may wish to the contrary, our parents remain our parents, no matter their age and no matter how old we get. And our parents never lose the obligation to teach us and shape who we are and how we handle relationships. They teach us about ourselves when we are young, and as they age, they teach us about the multigenerational task of giving wisdom to the family—how to negotiate the twists and turns of life, despite declining abilities and strength, and eventually how to die.

THE CRY FOR BLESSING

Most important, as our parents age, they pass the baton of adulthood and seniority to us through their blessing. This blessing comes most often not in some formal ceremony but when the parent looks at the adult child and in essence says, "You are a good person with great abilities. You are fully mature, you are fully adult, and I have confidence in you."

Of course, the blessing took on a more formal cast in Old Testament times. When Isaac knew his time was close, he summoned Esau and said, "I am now an old man and don't know the day of my death. Now then, get your weapons—your quiver and bow—and go out to the open country to hunt some wild game for me. Prepare me the kind of tasty food I like and bring it to me to eat, so that I may give you my blessing before I die" (Genesis 27:2–4).

Who knows what kind of father Isaac really was? Clearly, he played favorites and loved Esau more than he did Jacob. This had to hurt—and hurt has a way of multiplying itself. After Rebekah and Jacob schemed to get the blessing from Isaac, we see the desperation of Esau to gain his own blessing: "When Esau heard his father's words, he burst out with a loud and bitter cry and said to his father, 'Bless me—me too, my father!'" (Genesis 27:34).

In many ways, we adults who come from damaging families are still crying out for the same blessing. No matter what we like to think of ourselves in terms of our maturity and self-sufficiency, our parents remain our parents and continue to have a powerful influence on us. We know this deep down; that's why we desire their blessing. So despite their deep anger, Julie, Bill, and Bob showed up in my office to talk about Herb.

It is not so much a question of whether irresponsible older parents *deserve* our care; indeed, they do not. It is *their* burden and *their* irresponsibility that they have to carry, not ours. As Jeremiah 31:30 declares, they are responsible for their own sin, and their own teeth will be set on edge.

Our desire for fairness, peace, and blessing often drives us back into caregiving for and relationship with the irresponsible parent, even though we reason that we should cut off, forget, and obliterate that person's influence from our family legacy. Whether we like it or not, we remain tied to our parents and they remain smiths with the ability to hammer powerful blows—both positive and negative—on the metal of our personhood.

If we do not choose to address the unfairness, irresponsibility, and the lack of love (which we sometimes call "unfinished business"), we have a tendency to carry anger, bitterness, and hurt into other relationships. A great deal of damage can occur when we carry these unhealthy traits into relationships with our children, which in turn leaves them scarred and insecure.

But just because we choose to enter into a caregiving relationship with an older parent who has mistreated us in the past, it doesn't mean "anything goes." We must take on the caregiving task in a disciplined and responsible manner— one that gives the best chance for a loving and trustworthy relationship.

THERE IS ALWAYS FENCE WORK TO BE DONE

Out on the high plains of Texas, where keeping cattle where they belong is a major challenge, ranchers have a saying: "When everything else is finished, there is always fence work to be done."

In families with a history of irresponsibility and damaging interactions, the same principle holds true. There must be adequate stipulation of what issues belong to what people and strong boundaries about where others are not allowed to go. This is especially true of a family entering into a caregiving relationship that features unfinished business. There is always boundary work to be done.

Herb was eighty-three when doctors diagnosed him with a brain tumor. The day he arrived at my office for a family meeting, he hadn't seen all three of his children in the same place for more than forty years. As the oldest, Julie had borne the brunt of Herb's abuse. Understandably, she expressed hostility from the beginning.

"Well, now that you *have* to, you finally get in touch. How does it feel to be on the other end—needing something you won't get?"

Herb shot back. "You don't have any right to talk to me like that. I'm not asking one damn thing from you."

When people suffer from abusive relationships, they act like wounded animals that strike out viciously at anyone within reach. Because they are hurting, they threaten to hurt others. When an abused family gets together, the damage can escalate quickly. It's always necessary to draw boundaries to make sure damage stays at a minimum and escalation does not occur.

"One of the first things medical doctors learn," I said, "is first, do no harm. It basically means that, when treating a patient, you have to make sure you don't do things that will make him or her worse. We're here to talk about some very serious issues of care and some very harmful things that have happened in the past. One of the things I'd ask is that you give me permission to stop you when you are hurting one another."

Despite their anger, they all agreed to my request, while staring at the floor. Bill said, "OK, we aren't going to get anywhere by yelling at one another, so just tell us what we need to do, and we'll be done with it."

Herb scowled. Since Herb clearly had done some terrible things to his children and they were the ones who would provide his care, I wanted them to recognize the power of setting a boundary around their father.

"Before I ask any of you about a plan for Herb's care," I said, "I think it would be helpful to understand how you've been hurt in the past by this relationship. I find that if your father had the power to hurt you in a certain way in the past, he'll probably have the same power now."

Adult children who carry unfinished business around with them almost always fit such a profile. The older parent may not be able to physically abuse anyone, but he or she is still quite capable of saying or doing things that stab at the core of the previous damage.

"I want you to be able to stop Herb from ever hurting you again like he has in the past," I said.

Julie looked surprised and cynical at the same time. "Are you serious?" she asked. She proceeded to tell me many things, the crux of which amounted to Herb's desertion of his wife and children. Much of the adult burden left by his void had fallen on her shoulders as a child.

"I don't think it was all that bad for you," Herb said at one point, trying to minimize his irresponsibility.

"Herb," I replied immediately, "if you weren't around, you couldn't know how bad it was for her."

By rejecting Herb's statement and giving ear to Julie's complaint, we set the first of many boundaries.

Once a caregiver sets a boundary around the older person, it's necessary to learn the *sequence of interaction* that becomes destructive. Each hurtful relationship has a typical sequence of events, where one person does something and the other responds.

We fairly easily identified the sequence with Herb and Julie, since it had existed for years. Herb was a selfish man who would do whatever he wanted, from very menial things like watching a football game to extremely damaging things like going on a drinking binge. When Julie was young, Herb would pass his responsibility on to her by saying things like, "You don't need to play with your friends; you play with your brothers and keep an eye on them." As a child, Julie would try to please her father but would lose out on the things she wanted to do and then fail to receive any recognition or appreciation from her father. When her frustration with his irresponsibility peaked, she would explode. "They're *your* boys. *You* take care of them, you worthless bum!" Herb would then escalate the conflict. "You little prissy! You won't talk to *me* like that!" He then followed up by either physically abusing her or ignoring her and withdrawing. As he withdrew, more responsibility would fall on Julie, and the sequence would start all over again.

When Julie ignited the volley with her father—"How does it feel to be on the other end?"—Herb fell into the same abusive sequence of saying he wouldn't let her talk to him in such a manner. He was physically unable to hit her, but left unchecked, the two would have escalated, said more hurtful things, and then withdrawn. The sequence was alive and well. And it still had the power to cause Julie tremendous emotional pain.

Setting a boundary around these sequences means you find a point in the interaction where the relationship causes damage and then do something to stop the process. Instead of following the same hurtful path, you set a barrier in the path so the interaction has to go in another direction. I helped Julie recognize that the point where her father turned over his responsibility to her was the moment where the sequence became painful.

"You're right," she said, "it's always that moment when I buy into doing something that's *his* job that I lose."

It's amazing how difficult it is to set boundaries within a destructive situation. Most people have lived in the situation for so long they simply get used to the destructive pattern. It seems normal. For example, Sharon and I first realized we had to deal with Genevieve's alcoholism when a counselor pointed out how we were facilitating crazy behavior. When she'd drink too much before she came to dinner, we would change our plans or modify our conversation to suit her inebriated state. We would plan time into our schedule to check on her whenever she would stay at our house. When her anxiety grew out of control, we began asking the kids not to play on the swing set because it made her nervous. *We* acted crazy in response to her craziness. We didn't do it because we were stupid; we had simply been lulled into a bad pattern, a destructive habit. Families with very destructive patterns tend to fall into similar patterns and habits.

How might the sequence play out differently in Herb's family situation with boundaries in place? At the beginning of his cancer treatment, Herb had to visit a doctor twice a week for six weeks. Instead of *expecting* Julie to take him, he needed to be taught how to ask her so she could make a choice. Herb struggled to get the words out as we practiced together. "This is not your responsibility, but if you're willing, I need help getting to the doctor." I also practiced with Julie. Unless Herb actually asked her in an appropriate manner, without manipulation or demands, she was to say something like, "It's not my job to do what you are responsible for. You can't get help from me by demands. If you want me to consider helping you with your responsibilities, you'll have to ask in a different way." I then instructed her to withdraw.

Do boundaries work? Absolutely. Julie called me two days later with some news:

You won't believe what happened. Dad didn't call me to take him, so I did what you said and didn't pick him up. He called about fifteen minutes before his appointment and said, "You'd think you could remember to pick me up, since we just talked about it two days ago. You better get your tail in gear and get over here!" I felt the knife of his words and remembered that this was the exact place I needed that boundary. So I said to him, "It's not my job to take you to the doctor or anywhere else. If you want me to consider helping you, you'll have to ask me." I said good-bye and hung up the phone. God, it felt so freeing just to say something like that so straight without blowing my top! He called back in about five minutes, and do you know what he said? "I know it's not your job, but would you be willing to take me to the doctor?" I said yes. I picked him up and we didn't say much, but it's the first time I've been in my father's presence in years that I didn't feel like I wanted to tear his head off.

Herb and his son Bill had a different issue to deal with. Herb had hurt Bill primarily through his criticism. For example, Bill would go to the store for some of Herb's medical supplies, and then Herb would complain or chastise Bill for what he may have forgotten. Bill would feel hurt but just give up and withdraw. We worked in a similar fashion so that Bill would go to the store only if Herb expressed his appreciation.

Herb had to learn the hard way, but his children made excellent students. Because his care demanded a dramatic increase in the interaction between Herb and his children, several times over the next three weeks he ran into their boundaries after he acted in an unacceptable way. But he did learn. When Julie, Bill, and Bob began to realize they had enough power in the relationship to keep from being hurt repeatedly by Herb's actions, their anger started to diminish.

BUT IS IT CHRISTLIKE?

From time to time, someone will say to me, "These boundaries you suggest aren't very Christlike. They are so harsh."

On the contrary, I believe these types of boundaries are *exactly* Christlike. When the Pharisees of Jesus' day wanted to trip him up and put an end to his ministry, they followed him around, asking manipulative questions. One time, Jesus, who was committed to carrying out his Father's business of reconciling all of humanity to himself, responded, "A wicked and adulterous generation looks for a miraculous sign, but none will be given it except the sign of Jonah," and then he left and went away (Matthew 16:4).

Jesus, who came to build relationships and make reconciliation possible between humanity and God, clearly recognized the Pharisees' tactics. I don't believe he was being harsh with them as much as he was telling them what it would take to do business with him. It was as though he said, "I won't allow you to waste my time or frustrate my ministry. You get honest with yourselves and get your motives right, and then you'll be ready to talk with me."

In the same way, setting boundaries in order to keep from being damaged by old sequences is a necessary first step to take old and harmful patterns in a new direction. It provides a way to fulfill our responsibilities as caregivers to our older parents without subjecting ourselves to further damage from them. It stops the abuse, but it also opens up the opportunity and possibility that a more positive relationship can develop.

For some, setting boundaries with the older parent and stopping painful sequences are the only unfinished pieces of business that can be accomplished. It is important to remember, however, that every person has a story. People are usually not mean, manipulative, or abusive for no reason. And the stories of our irresponsible parents are also worth hearing.

It Was Worse for Him Than It Was for Us

We all cry out for understanding when life treats us unfairly. If my mother physically abused me, then others should understand why I have a bad temper. If I grew up in a cold and emotionally sterile home, then people should cut me some slack for not being a touchy-feely person.

But while we may find it easy to expect understanding from others when we suffer at the hands of damaging or irresponsible parents, we often find it extremely difficult to extend the same understanding to others.

After we had established some boundaries for Herb, I inquired about his own personal history.

"You don't want to hear, and I'm not sure I want to remember," he said.

"Your past has helped make you who you are, just as some of the past has contributed to making Julie, Bill, and Bob who they are," I replied. "I've listened to their sides of the story, and now I want to hear yours."

I'm used to hearing about damaging childhoods, but Herb's story was more brutal than usual. He was the oldest of three boys, and his father was a raging alcoholic ever since Herb could remember. His father would take the money he had earned at his infrequent periods of work at the cotton mill and spend it on alcohol, forcing Herb and his mother to beg for food from neighbors. When his father would come home from a binge, he would pick a fight with Herb's mother and physically abuse her and the boys. This situation continued until Herb was fourteen and felt old enough to take on his "old man."

"I'd had enough," Herb said, "and so once when he came home drunk, I told him to get out. I told him that if he ever touched my mother again, I'd kill him. He took a swing at me and cussed me. I grabbed a stick we poked the fire with and slammed it across his head. He staggered back and out the door. I felt pretty good about myself and felt like that had put an end to it."

Herb got much quieter as he finished the story. "About ten minutes later," he continued, "he came in with a pistol and fired up into the ceiling. He grabbed me and pistol-whipped me until I was unconscious. He beat me up bad enough that he was sent to prison for a while. I was in the hospital for about three weeks. After he got out of jail, he would just stare at me. I really never knew when he was going to go for me next, and I was sure he would try to kill me. My mother wouldn't leave him, so I decided to leave myself."

"How old were you?" I asked.

"I was fifteen," he answered. "I grew up pretty rough and never saw my family again."

I asked Herb's children if they had ever heard the story, and they replied that they had known he had left home when he was a teenager but never really knew why. Bob commented, "As bad as it was, it was worse for him than it was for us." Julie quickly pointed out, "That may be true, but it's no excuse for what he did to us."

For many, trying to understand any part of an abuser's history sounds like an excuse for inexcusable behavior and seems to let him or her off the hook. Actually, I think it does just the opposite. Human beings have complex histories, and many things contribute to their personalities and actions. Irresponsible or abusive humans are not monsters. Monsters kill and maim simply because that is what they are made to do. If we label Hitler or Stalin as monsters, then they lie beyond the reach of responsibility. Only human beings can be held responsible for their actions; only human beings can be held responsible for how they shape their children and treat their families. I can insist an abuser is wrong and irresponsible, and yet still try to understand how he or she became such a person. I can also express understanding of and empathy toward his or her limitations and background and believe that he or she must make amends for the wrongs committed.

So if such understanding does not alleviate responsibility, what *does* it do? It connects us—human being to human being. Most of us who have caused great pain in our families are not monsters or fiends; we are human beings who make mistakes. And when I, as a human being, put myself in the shoes of my abuser and seek to understand his or her circumstances of development, limitations, or history, I conclude that, given the same environment, I may have made the same mistakes. It's easier to take responsibility when those around us do not treat us as though we were wild beasts.

For those damaged by irresponsible parents, such understanding can reduce the pain and anguish over the past. Herb's story, for example, clearly moved Julie, Bill, and Bob. No one in the room uttered platitudes like, "That's OK," or, "I'm glad you told me." A moment of clarity arrived, and everyone in the room shared a history of victimization—which meant that they shared not only common feelings but also common ways in which they had acted irresponsibly in relationships.

There is no magic formula to gain such understanding. All it takes is a caregiver willing to get in touch with his or her own fallibility and a willingness to go prospecting for the story.

If you have an older parent who is difficult, manipulative, or abusive, realize that there is a story behind who he or she is. Understanding will not alleviate responsibility or even make everything OK. It will, however, tie you together with your older parent in a way that yields common ground and at the same time reduces the amount of pain and resentment you feel.

THERE IS A CHANCE IT MAY BE FIXABLE

I've been around many caregivers who have punishing, abusive, and manipulative older parents. They often feel as though they have an albatross around their necks. They do not like caregiving, and they do not like their older parents. They wish the pain in the neck would just go away. Many of these people refuse to take any risk that may lead to some redemption of the relationship.

People give several reasons for feeling this way. "My mother can't change. She's been like this all her life, and it is just hopeless," I often hear. I have worked with aging families for more than twenty years now, and I can honestly make this assertion: I have *never* met an older person unable to change. To be sure, not all older people do change, but the mythology of "You can't teach an old dog new tricks" is simply that—a myth. Most times, I find that this notion is caregiver code for "My parent is a pain, and I don't want to go to the effort to find out if he or she will change." Often this means it is the *caregiver* who is unwilling to give change a try. He or she refuses to let go of grudges or anger.

Fear and guilt cause other caregivers to refuse to take the risk of confronting old parental habits: "My father is so old I'm afraid that if I brought up any issues of the past, it might kill him. I just don't think I could live with such guilt." The reality is that our older parents will die, *regardless* of the issues that are brought up. It also seems odd that, while the older parent has been irresponsible or mean, *we* are the ones who feel guilty if we speak up about it and accept the pain for the rest of our lives. Fear and guilt in these situations usually result from the abuse or damage caused by the older parent. It may feel like emotional gridlock, but we should at least be willing to make *some* moves.

In some families, setting boundaries and limiting damage is the best that can be achieved; others can limit damage and begin to understand each other's histories and development. But in some families—even when heinous abuse has occurred—there remains the possibility of reconciliation. When I say "reconciliation," I don't mean letting go of past wrongs as much as I mean putting love and trust back into the relationship. It means that the older person has a chance to make amends for past violations of love and trust. This kind of reconciliation represents the pinnacle of forgiveness— where we come back into right relationship with one another.

How is it possible that a caregiver in his or her forties, fifties, or sixties, who has suffered decades of abuse by a parent who has now grown old and has serious health issues, could experience such a reconciliation? It never ceases to amaze me the funny things God does with human beings in space and time. As I write this, I'm a grown man in my late forties. Yet some memories and emotions of when I was eight years old feel just as pristine to me as the day they occurred. In some ways, that eight-year-old boy is still inside of me. I'm not speaking of the "inner child" so much as the truth that we are an accumulation of everything that has happened in our personal history. Just like a tree, the original "stuff" of the sapling is there in the hundred-year-old oak. The tree grows upward but never moves from the original location of the sapling. And since that "child" is still available, all the issues, violations, and questions of that child can still be addressed. In the same way, the parent remains the parent throughout our lifetime and, as such, still has the ability to address the past injustices.

Herb would have died an emotionally poorer man had not someone raised the possibility of doing something different. His children would gladly have let him die and probably been overjoyed that he had passed out of their hair forever—without ever realizing he had the water that could quench their thirst for love. But the work that Julie, Bill, and Bob did on setting boundaries, combined with the understanding they had forged with Herb, produced an opportunity for reconciliation.

After six weeks of treatment, doctors had done all they could to stem the progression of the tumor in Herb's brain. He was referred to hospice and started his final march toward death. We had met together on four occasions. Herb's children were helping primarily with getting him to appointments, bringing in medical supplies, and checking in on him nearly every day. But all the heavy caregiving—feeding, bathing, and medication supervision—fell to me and my staff. As Herb declined and I knew it'd be the last time we would meet, I asked some questions that gave the family an opportunity to make things different.

"The end for Herb is in the very near future," I said to Julie, Bill, and Bob. "If this were the last time you would see your father, what would be the one thing you'd most like to have answered?" All three children got that faraway stare to the right side of the floor—the stare you get when you look into the window of past emotions and your deepest longings.

"I guess I'd like to know if you ever thought what you did to us was wrong," Julie said, looking at her father. He thought for a long time. You could see the competition going on inside of him, like a furious table tennis match. Should he be defensive or straight with her? Finally he answered.

"I always knew I was wrong," Herb said. "I just was too much of a jackass to admit what I was doing to all of you."

In family therapy work, you never know whether people will accept the opportunities to change that get offered. When they do, you feel the same happy release of anxiety you felt as a child when you were sure a ferocious killer had come into your room at night, only to find out it was your parent leaving you a present. The confession encouraged Bill to ask, "Did you love us?"

Herb paused for a long time and finally said, "To tell the truth, I don't know. I don't know that I ever knew exactly what love was. I do know this. I do know I love you now."

Tears were trickling down several faces, and after several minutes, I looked at Herb and said, "You've gone this far and maybe you'd be willing to go a little further. The past has been damaging to you and you have been damaging to your children. If you know you love them now, maybe you could ask forgiveness for the past and commit to loving them for the time you have left." I suggested, as I had many times, that Herb make the impact of his forgiveness request more powerful by asking on his knees.

Herb struggled down to the ground and grabbed the hands of his three children. "I've been a hard man. I've done you kids wrong, and I know that now. You don't have to give it, but I want to ask for your forgiveness for all I've done to you—the things I haven't done for you. I wish I could have loved you then like I love you now." He glanced up into Julie's eyes as he spoke the last words. Julie leaned forward, put her arms around his neck, and whispered, "Oh, Daddy."

Some people may think it mean or unkind to get an eighty-three-year-old man down on his knees to ask forgiveness from his three adult children whom he abused. I think not.

I think of the differences between the biblical story about the rich man (Luke 16) and Jesus' interaction with the woman at the well (John 4). The rich man, after he neglected Lazarus and was sent to the place of torment, asked that a messenger be sent to his living brothers so they could avoid such a horrible fate. He made no request for himself, for it was too late for him to change; change is reserved for the living. On the other hand, after Jesus forced the woman at the well to confront her sinful past, the Master also gave her the opportunity to begin living differently.

As caregivers, we all carry cuts, bruises, and minor scars from our histories with our parents. Some, however, live with severed limbs and terminal diseases caused by irresponsible and damaging parents. When those of us who have these severe issues are called on to care for the older parent, it hardly seems fair to give care that is not deserved. But it is possible and necessary to do the job of caregiving, even in the context of difficult circumstances. It takes discipline, patience, and a willingness to start over again and again—but it is possible.

Julie, Bill, and Bob took over more and more of Herb's care in the final weeks of his life. I recall the last time I saw Herb, about one week before he died. He was lying on his bed, and Bill and Bob were on opposite sides of the bed, holding his hands. Julie was sitting on the bed, stroking his head of chalk-white hair. The caregivers were getting the care they had always longed for. And there was peace.

UNFINISHED BUSINESS AND PEACE

I hate yard work. Once, when I was dashing around trying to finish the lawn on what I call a "quick mow," I ran into a tree branch that deposited an inch-long thorn into one of my biceps. The thorn broke off, but from my vantage point, I couldn't tell if the thorn still remained or had just created a wound. After failing to find the thorn, I assumed that, while it had punctured the skin, it had not stayed in my arm.

I was wrong.

The wound quickly healed, at least on the outside. Day to day, it caused me no discomfort and very little thought. But every now and again, something bumped my arm in just the right place, and once again I felt the stab of the thorn buried deep in my skin. So it was there after all. But how best to treat the wound? Most of the time it gave me no problems. If I tried to remove it, would the result be any more desirable than the present discomfort?

Our elders often cause us deep pain from long-ago wounds. They caused most of them out of ignorance, not malice. Still, the wounding happened just the same. Caregiving puts us close to the person and bumps our thorn in just the right place, so that it hurts all over again. And we don't know whether broaching the old issue will do us any good. And even if it would, how would we ever go about getting started? Finishing unfinished business is difficult work—but it is worth the effort.

On the walls of the American Museum of Natural History in New York City, visitors find several quotes from President Theodore Roosevelt. "If I must choose between righteousness and peace," one quote says, "I choose righteousness." I believe the two must go together. If we pursue righteousness as a "just and holy cause," we will tend to act harshly and misuse power in the name of right. If we pursue peace alone, we will tend to adopt an appeasement policy—the same kind that proved to be a profound failure in the days before World War II. Appeasement of a tyrant only encourages the tyrant to abuse more. Only when we courageously take up the power of a righteous cause, governed by our desire for reconciliation and peace, will we find truly balanced and nurturing relationships.

We set boundaries to stop damaging interactions—not to punish an older parent but because it is right and it offers the best opportunity for change. But we seek understanding and reconciliation also because the opportunity to love and make peace remains alive as long as the day lasts.

QUESTIONS FOR CONSIDERATION

1. If you have a damaging or manipulative older parent, what sequences of interaction often result in hurt or angry escalation?

2. What major events, limitations, and developmental issues shaped the life and personality of your older parent? If you had grown up in his or her place, do you think you would have done better than your older parent did? Why?

3. What is the crux of the past hurts and pains you wish your older parent could address? Who could help you explore the possibility of reconciliation?

PART 2

Embracing the Work of Caregiving

We work hard with our own hands. When we are cursed, we bless; when we are persecuted, we endure it; when we are slandered, we answer kindly. Up to this moment we have become the scum of the earth, the refuse of the world.

1 Corinthians 4:12–13

Medicare. Doctors. Medications. Advanced directives. Living wills. What does it take to stand up to the rigors of caregiving?

It is certainly a job very few of us trained for in school. It's like being apprenticed to do a job without the benefit of a master craftsman to teach us. Many times, it feels as though we are left on our own to sink or swim. And what do we get for all our efforts to learn, control, and manage? Some of us receive appreciation—sometimes. But some of the time we receive curses, persecutions, and slanders, most often from the very people we are trying to help most.

You may hear these phrases:
- "You don't care about me."
- "Why are you so mean?"
- "You're trying to cheat us out of what is ours."
- "Leave me alone."

You did not sign up for this kind of treatment.

But we actually do have a master craftsman to whom we are apprenticed. The medical, financial, and legal morass actually presents us with opportunities to become molded into the character God desires. It's confusing work, but it's something we can learn how to do—work that can contribute significantly to our spiritual growth.

3

Aging and the Way
We Were Not

Since my youth, O God, you have taught me,
and to this day I declare your marvelous deeds.
Even when I am old and gray,
do not forsake me, O God,
till I declare your power to the next generation,
your might to all who are to come.
Psalm 71:17–18

Most of us have some image in our mind's eye of what a family should look like. We see a home with a runway of green grass and trees as big as clouds. We envision a loving and nurturing stay-at-home mother, a hardworking and responsible father, and children who do their chores and play for long hours with the neighbors. The family eats dinner together, has long conversations together, and takes summer vacations that bag a boatload of memories.

Most likely our image of "family" includes only parents and children. Only rarely does someone's idea of family include a multigenerational household—and rarer still does it include caregiving for an older person.

When I speak to groups and bring up this fact, inevitably someone comments on the tragedy of how our culture treats older people. He or she will speak about how we tend to put away our older people and how families used to care for their aged at home. Most of us have an image of a time when families seemed much closer than they are today, when grandparents had a vital part in their children's and grandchildren's lives. When it came time for Grandma or Grandpa to die, they died in the family house, in their own bed and surrounded by several generations of family.

These are nice images and nice ideas. The problem is, they don't represent how the family is or how the family was. When these false images turn into "facts," we tend to hold ourselves to unreasonable (if not impossible) standards that tend to increase our guilt and frustration.

Such was the case when Alice came to see me to "get some direction on how to handle Mom."

I FEEL SO GUILTY

Alice was a vigorous sixty-six-year-old, married to Harry, who was sixty-eight. They had three adult children and seven grandchildren. Life seemed very good for the couple as Alice retired from teaching and Harry wrapped up his career with the postal service. They planned to travel a bit, volunteer in their community and church, and enjoy their growing extended family.

Then Alice's aged mother came back into her life, needing care.

"She's always lived fairly independently, except that she's overweight," said Alice. "Last spring, she had more and more trouble getting around. The doctors said her heart is enlarged and she's on the path of heart disease. In the last month, she has stopped driving and shopping for herself, and I have to insist everyday that she bathe and brush her teeth." Alice sighed heavily. "All of a sudden, my life revolves around my mother's needs," she continued. "I hate to say it, but I'm a little resentful of the fact that I'm losing the life I thought I would have—you know, seeing my grandchildren and enjoying my retirement. Now it feels like I have another child to take care of. My mother is a wonderful person. I feel so guilty about even saying I resent taking care of her."

Guilt and frustration have nothing to offer in the job of effective caregiving. These evil twins will sap our energies and put us on paths that not only destroy our family relationships but also our relationship with God.

Yet caregiving is a job that must be done. If we are to face the task of caregiving from a relational and family perspective, we must bear in mind some truths about aging—current and past. Correct images of family and caregiving will help us be realistic instead of frustrated, loving instead of guilty.

GROWING OLD: THE TIMES, THEY ARE A'CHANGIN'

How did we get so many older people? And are there actually more older people today than in previous generations?

Aging has changed dramatically throughout the last century. More than ever, we need an accurate picture of how these changes affect the challenges we face. We can get this picture in two ways: first, by understanding the increase in the older population; and second, by understanding the issues older people face.

How our world has changed in just a century! It was only a hundred years ago that the Wright brothers made the first powered air flight, for a grand total of twelve seconds. Today, jumbo jets carry hundreds of passengers over entire oceans on ten-hour flights. This same kind of remarkable change in longevity has occurred in the United States. In 1900, the average life span was a little over forty-seven years; today, people can expect to live, on average, to a little under seventy-seven—almost a thirty-year increased life span in a century!

The United States has significantly more older people today than a century ago. In 1900, only about 3 million people (4 percent of the population) was over age sixty-five. Now, almost 40 million Americans are over sixty-five—about 13 percent of the population. The fastest-growing age group, by percentage of population, for the last three censuses is the group aged eighty-five and older. This means that the oldest of the old, who are likely to be the folks in need of the most care, are increasing the fastest.

Of course, this increase is only part of the story. Most of the people who make up the present aging population were born in the 1920s and 1930s—a time of a relatively low birth rate due to a devastating economic depression. In the next twenty years, the real tidal wave of aging population will occur when the baby boomers of the 1940s and 1950s will retire. Almost 70 million people over the age of sixty-five are expected by the year 2030. Our children will face much more of a caregiving job, so they'll watch carefully how we handle the current situation.

There is also a substantial difference in the gender makeup of the older population. On average, women live longer than men—one reason being that male hormones take a greater toll on physical longevity. As a result, there are about eighty-three males to every hundred females between the ages of sixty-five and seventy. The imbalance increases with age. By the time people reach age eighty-five, there are only forty males to every hundred females. We are not only a graying nation, we are more and more a graying *feminine* nation.

Why do people live so much longer? Medical advances in treating and curing acute diseases are primarily responsible for the increase. Well into the twentieth century, the number one cause of death in the United States was influenza and pneumonia, with the very young and very old most at risk. Today, very few die of such acute problems. What's more, medical treatment keeps people alive today in situations where only thirty years ago there was no chance of cure. When I was a kid growing up in the 1960s, it wasn't unusual for men to have heart attacks and die in their fifties or sixties. Nowadays, most of these men can take medications or have surgeries, so only rarely does a man die of heart disease while in his sixties. Modern medicine has made a phenomenal difference—but as we've seen in recent years, medications and treatments are not cheap.

Increased longevity has significant implications for the way we "do family." When I was a boy, I remember our local paper coming to our house to take a picture of five generations of females in my family, starting with my great-grandmother and ending with my sister's daughter. Today, five-generation family complexes are almost commonplace. Most of the current generation of caregivers in their sixties saw their grandparents die long before their parents retired. Like Alice, they are awakening to the fact that, just at the time they thought their lives would slow down, they have to care for their parents who are in their eighties.

Combine this with another sociological change. It now takes the average person longer to separate from his or her parents' home and financial support. Many parents are helping or partially supporting their children and their children's young families well into their offspring's mid- to late-twenties. This has become especially true for parents whose adult female children are divorced with children; often the adult child must move back in to survive. In many of these situations, the grandparents become the major caregivers to the grandchildren. Thus, we have what is called the "sandwich generation," a phrase coined to describe the generation that has caregiving and support responsibilities both to their aging parents and to their young adult children.

What does all this mean? Perhaps it's dawning on you that there are more older people in need of help and more younger adults still in need of help, and the resources are more expensive—and you, as a caregiver, find yourself in the middle of a demographic whirlwind. You are the baloney in the sandwich generation!

Most of us will be giving care at an age long past the time we got our first AARP card and well into the time we'll be counted among the aging population. As I said before, we all age, but we don't all need care. Remember, I use the term "older parents" to describe those who can no longer provide for their own care and who need regular assistance from family. Most of what we call the "aging population" is actually *middle-aging*, meaning they carry on with fairly normal activities and provide care for themselves and others.

With that said, when a person is really old and in need of care, it almost always means something is medically wrong. Today, being old usually means we live with *chronic* disease as opposed to *terminal* disease. An older person may live for years with diabetes, heart disease, emphysema, or high blood pressure. Medicine has made these problems manageable, although not curable. Most people over the age of seventy are on at least three or more medications. When we are old, we do live longer—but often with some measure of health impairment.

Another aspect of growing old is living with loss. When a person is really old, his or her world begins to shrink. In most cases, the older person's spouse has died, and many of his or her friends have either passed away or are in need of care themselves. Many of his or her physical capabilities have deteriorated and thus have to be compensated for by family or others. Many older people will have cognitive losses that require someone to either help with or take over financial responsibilities and decision making. Since older people typically aren't in the workforce, their financial security is on the wane. Some will lose their houses as they have to move closer to family or into a care facility. These are tremendous losses that can make growing old a devastating and depressing time of life.

In short, when an older person comes under your care, the job can be both substantial and burdensome. Although most of us will negotiate the transition into caregiving, nevertheless there are stresses related to time management, responding to physical or cognitive needs of the older person, financial problems, decision making, planning for the future, and resolving feelings of guilt and inadequacy, just to name a few. As a result, caregivers can experience physical illnesses, increased depression, and lower life satisfaction, and they may age prematurely themselves.

Make no mistake, caregiving can be hazardous to your health. It can be a burdensome task. Like Alice, the reality of an older parent requiring our care can blow apart our ready-made plans of how we thought we would spend a good portion of our lives. Even when we come to grips with the task of caregiving, many of us will suffer from inadequacies or the feeling that we're letting down our older parents or the rest of our families. These are the realities we must face as we get on with the task ahead.

THE BIBLE AND CAREGIVING

While the Bible often uses the phrase "growing old," it has little in common with the modern experience. In the book of Genesis, for example, we are introduced to a chorus of characters who lived spectacularly long lives. Adam lived to be 930; Seth was 912; Enosh, 905; and so on, up to Methuselah, who lived a grand total of 969 years. I'm not quite sure what to think about all these reports of people who lived several centuries, but I do find it interesting that some researchers in aging believe they have discovered genetic codes that cause the aging process. Some of these researchers speculate that, by manipulating these codes, there is no reason why humans couldn't live for five hundred years. While I find the thought intriguing, this kind of information has absolutely no impact on my experience in the here and now. A few of us will have experiences with people who live to be a hundred and more, but it will be by far the exception.

The next theme in Genesis concerning aging is seen in the way God uses old people to set in motion his plan of redemption. Most notable is the story of Abraham and Sarah. God promises that Abraham will have many descendants, and to drive the point home that it's God's power that will create the nation, the Lord waits until Abraham and Sarah are well advanced in age. Abraham is nearly one hundred years old when Isaac is conceived, and Sarah is so old she considers the divine promise a joke! "So Sarah laughed to herself as she thought, 'After I am worn out and my master is old, will I now have this pleasure?'" (Genesis 18:12).

Again, these stories are interesting, and I believe they show the power and faithfulness of God. But the story doesn't help me much when I'm trying to understand aging, as I've never seen any ninety-year-old, first-time parents.

Finally, the book of Genesis talks about old age when it comes time for the great characters of the story to die. The phrase "old and full of years" (or related phrases) appears again and again in describing the demise of Abraham, Isaac, Jacob, and Joseph (see Genesis 25:8; 35:29). While this is a good epitaph and a worthy goal, it does not reveal much about how to give care successfully in my day and time. In fact, we find no direct guidance on caregiving for the elderly in the whole of Scripture. So, in the face of all these changes regarding life span and an aging population, how do I find help from the Bible on how to give care for my older parent?

THREE BIBLICAL PRINCIPLES

Here are three biblical principles I find instructive:

Responsibility

Within the command "Honor your father and your mother, so that you may live long in the land the LORD your God is giving you" (Exodus 20:12) lies the principle of *responsibility*.

At first blush, the command may appear straightforward. God tells us to honor our parents by listening to what they say, respecting who they are, and caring for their needs. In return for our obedience, things will go well for us. While I believe these things are true, I suspect the passage has a much deeper meaning.

One weekend, my wife, Sharon, was out of town, and so the job of bathing my mother-in-law, Genevieve, fell to me. I was clumsy with the job, and despite her Alzheimer's, Genevieve somehow recognized my struggle to overcome modesty, my discomfort with making her do something she dreaded, and my desire to escape the responsibility. As I began to help her into the tub, she said, "You aren't doing it right, but I guess we will make it OK." Even though she didn't like the process any more than I, she let me care for her and accepted my mistakes. As we went through the process, it was as though all my discomfort got washed away. Instead of a chore, it became one of the sweeter times with Genevieve as we shared a common task. I tried to assist her with getting clean physically, and she helped me to get cleaner emotionally.

The fact is, we will have to perform tasks that the older person does not want and claims he or she does not need. If Genevieve would have screamed at me, which she sometimes does, "Stop it! You are being mean to me. Now do what I say," would I have dishonored her to continue? I don't think so. The job of bathing has to be done, regardless of her desire. But if we perform the disagreeable task with an attitude of respect, sincerely do what we think is best, and consider what our older parent desires, I believe we can safely say we are honoring him or her. This is the deeper meaning of the command. If our older parents join in the process, they don't have to be happy or approving, but they do have to be respectful and malleable.

To give care is our responsibility, but it requires cooperation between caregiver and older person. We form a braided cord with our older parent, tied at one end to the here and now and at the other to emotional well-being in the future. We honor, work with, and stay connected to our older parents because in this way we demonstrate to our children and future generations the essential quality and value of relationships. Relationships grow over the decades by drill and by following the command to march. We do not learn much about ourselves through short and shallow relationships, because when things get difficult, we simply cut them off and move on. God intends our family relationships to grow long and deep so that we may learn the discipline of confronting ourselves and the wisdom of our family histories. When we honor our parents, we demonstrate the necessary components that keep us connected to one another.

This is what the command means by the promise of long days. Many people honored their parents but had short lives and premature deaths. It is not so much a promise for long life as a promise that working together in relationships keeps our family members connected to one another and, in reality, connected to God.

It is our responsibility to honor our parents and thus give care to them when they grow old. But let us be clear what that responsibility means. It does not mean that an older parent has the right to demand anything or treat offspring in a disrespecting way, and the caregiver just has to take it; it does not mean that if the caregiver does exactly what the parent says, he or she automatically gets God's blessing of a long life. It means that the honor, respect, and cooperation between parent and child demonstrates how to humbly work together for future generations, and it reminds us how we are expected to do the same in our relationship to God. We honor our parents not so much for their benefit (and certainly not so much for ours) but for the benefit of showing our children how to stay connected to family. This is what makes for long family lines and for living long in the land. Our responsibility to honor our parents results in the type of rewarding connection I felt in bathing Genevieve.

Openhandedness

A verse in Deuteronomy suggests the second principle I find helpful in caring for an older parent: "If there is a poor man among your brothers in any of the towns of the land that the LORD your God is giving you, do not be hardhearted or tightfisted toward your poor brother. Rather be openhanded and freely lend him whatever he needs" (Deuteronomy 15:7–8). The Bible is replete with commands on how to care for someone in need, but I believe this one speaks to our day and time better than any other. I like it so much because it speaks of refusing to be tightfisted but instead having an attitude of *openhandedness*.

Alice is like so many of us who have the burden of caregiving handed to us. We had other plans and other responsibilities that occupied our minds and hearts. Yet all of a sudden, an older parent consumes more and more of our time and energies, leaving our other desires and responsibilities to be pushed to the back burner. And let's be honest: one of the really difficult things about giving all this time and energy to the job of caregiving is that, at least in the long run, it does no good. Our needy parents may have ups and downs, but overall they are on a downward trajectory. They will deteriorate and eventually die. Caregiving, for the most part, is not like building emotionally close times with a spouse or making memories with grandchildren. Sometimes it may feel as though we're sending all our energies down a black hole.

This may be why the picture we build in our mind's eye of what family life should be can cause us so much grief. When we build such images, we begin to think it's our right to have our dream. American culture certainly encourages this perspective. Alice struggled hard with this as she thought about caring for her mother.

"I love my mother, but I had so many dreams about how my husband and I would enjoy life," she said. "We both had to work so hard to give our kids the things they wanted, and I always felt guilty I didn't have more time to enjoy them when they were kids. Then when they were older, they were doing their own things, and we had to work hard to get them through college. But I told myself that when we retired, we'd have time to enjoy one another and enjoy them. Now with Mother, it is just one more time my dreams get moved to the back burner. I look at several of my friends who are traveling and enjoying their grandkids, and I can't help but be resentful that *I'm* the one who is stuck."

I assured Alice that her feelings were not unusual. They represent a struggle we all have at different points. "Any time we begin to form the idea of what we expect or what we deserve," I said, "we have a tendency to start holding on to it and protecting it. There's nothing wrong with wanting time with your husband or desiring to be a fun grandmother, but there is a difference in thinking it's your *right* instead of looking for how it fits with the reality of your job of caregiving."

The priest and renowned Christian writer Henri Nouwen spent many of the last years of his life living in a L'Arche community in Toronto. In this community, a caregiver is given charge of one individual with severe special needs, and the special needs individual is given charge of the caregiver. In one of two conversations I had with Henri, I asked him, "How do you keep giving and giving in that situation?" With a look of surprise on his face, Henri said, "I never think about it that way. It isn't like I have something to protect or hold and I give it out. Whatever the situation is at that time in life, God will give me the grace to do what I need to do at the time and to receive what I need to at the time." In other words, life is fluid and isn't to be held close to the vest. As long as we don't try in a tightfisted way to hold on to what we have and instead try to take life as it is, we will be (and will become) adequate to the task of responding to the needs around us.

I told Alice, "I think all of us desire to have life the way we want it, but I think God wants us to hold what happens in an openhanded way. When we are openhanded, we give what is necessary to our parents—but when we have the same open hand, we're also able to receive what God is giving to us or teaching us. I think that's the key in thinking about the job you face. Caregiving is part of your life now. It isn't about what we are missing but more about what we're learning and receiving from the process of the give-and-take of life."

This made sense to Alice. "I think I do fall into that trap of trying to protect my life from my mother and then resenting what I've lost," she said. "I think I just need to face what needs to be done each day and just do it instead of worrying about everything I've lost."

Evenness

I see the final principle for caregiving in two Bible passages from the gospel of Luke: "Yet the news about him spread all the more, so that crowds of people came to hear him and to be healed of their sicknesses. But Jesus often withdrew to lonely places and prayed" (Luke 5:15–16). The needs around Jesus seemed both overwhelming and right in front of him, yet he took time to nurture his own spiritual relationship.

In the second passage, Jesus spoke to a would-be follower who said he wanted to become a disciple but first had to go and bury his father. Jesus told him, "Let the dead bury their own dead, but you go and proclaim the kingdom of God" (Luke 9:60). The Lord's words aren't as harsh as they might seem. He meant something like this: "There is work to be done in the kingdom of God—work that is different from the work done in the family."

In these two Bible excerpts, I find the principle of balance, or what I call *evenness*.

My wife alternates between laughing at and being annoyed with one of my bigger character faults. Whenever something goes wrong around the house—whether it be a noise in the car, the washing machine on the blink, or a spot on the carpet—I stop whatever I'm doing and take a look. It doesn't matter if Sharon and I are in the midst of an important conversation or deeply involved in another project; the new problem immediately gets bumped to the head of the line and gets my full attention until it is solved.

Many of us are problem solvers, though you may not match my intensity. This presents a problem in caregiving, because a constant string of needs and challenges seemingly all have to be addressed. If we respond to the immediate problem and try to solve it, our whole life can easily be consumed by the job.

God does want us to take on the responsibility of caring for our parents and does want us to be openhanded in our giving, but he also wants us to achieve balance. There are other things in our lives and in his kingdom that must be done. Living successfully means we are even and balanced in the way we live life.

Alice struggled with this problem. She felt that if her mother had a need, she had to respond immediately. "Now that my mom needs care," she said, "I find I can't get it out of my mind.

I'm always thinking what needs to be done next and how I should be checking on her. If I try to do something for myself or spend time with my family, I worry and feel guilty."

"You have other things in your life that need to be done," I responded. "If you continue to work to take care of your mother until all the problems are solved, then you will be a full-time caregiver. There will always be problems in aging, just as there will always be poor people among us."

Alice and I worked to find some of the origins of her guilt. She was an overachiever, and, like so many in our culture, she derived good feelings about herself from the way she performed her tasks. Alice was willing to work on these issues, which would greatly reduce her guilt, but she also had to come to grips with some problems that couldn't be solved or had to be solved by others.

"It's hard for me to let things go," she said, "but I'm beginning to see that it's not the end of the world if Mom's teeth aren't brushed every day and that I have to trust it's OK for my husband to check on her or go shopping for her."

Alice eventually began to learn that caregiving had to be integrated into her whole life, along with being a wife, mother, grandmother, and friend. God gives us all these roles and all our responsibilities for a reason. Many times we don't see what the reason might be, but we can be assured it's all meant for our growth as people of God. He doesn't mean for us to spend our lives exclusively in caregiving, so we must learn how to nurture and fulfill the other aspects of our lives and let some demands remain undone or be reserved for a later time.

So many problems in life occur when people become too focused on one or two things. When I think of these principles of responsibility, openhandedness, and evenness, I see that the three work in balance. I cannot be consumed by responsibility toward Genevieve without letting some of my other obligations go. I cannot give and give to Genevieve exclusively, because I have others to whom I must give. Life demands a constant balance, and therefore a constant tension exists to balance these three principles. Almost always, I find that following the example of Jesus produces this type of tension.

When Genevieve was in the early moderate stage of her Alzheimer's, she could still attend worship and adult Sunday school. Of all the things I love to do, teaching stands at the top of my list. It is my one best thing. Through the years, I've almost always taught an adult Sunday school class; it has been water to my thirsty soul. When I taught, Sharon would sit with Genevieve, and then we'd all go to the worship service.

As our youngest son entered middle school, Sharon began to feel the call to teach his Sunday school class. I encouraged her because I thought it would be a fulfilling experience, but I also thought it would be a good break from all that Sharon was doing for her mom—from handling all the finances, to bathing her, to making all of her doctor's appointments. I was hoping Genevieve would sit quietly during my lesson. And she did sit on the front row during my teaching—for a while. But more and more, she would get agitated. Church was the last of the social activities Genevieve could negotiate, and she clung to it like a wasp to flypaper.

I decided, for at least a season of my life, to give up teaching my class. My ministry at church became picking Genevieve up, getting some coffee for her, sitting with her in my old Sunday school class, and helping her negotiate the worship service. Did I miss teaching? You bet. But I felt an undeniable rhythm of rightness in honoring her by helping her attend church, learning from the openhanded privilege of serving her, and knowing I was giving up teaching only for a while as we negotiated this phase of Genevieve's disease. Following the biblical principles of caregiving always involves finding this rhythm of rightness.

THE POWER OF THE POWERLESS

When it works properly, caregiving is a great blessing. It is a blessing, not only because it teaches us the humility necessary to look at ourselves honestly but also because it teaches us about the grace of true, unconditional love.

The practice of caregiving has a sanctifying effect in honing our personal lives as well as in giving us an appreciation for the experience of yielding to another human being. These spiritual lessons are hard to learn in a rich, materialistic society that seeks to protect us from much of life's messiness.

But in order to get the blessing of caregiving, we depend on the one receiving the care. In a very real sense, we depend on those who depend on us. For if our older parent is unwilling to receive our care, we get locked into a battle that can win no territory. Our lives can be changed by caregiving, but it depends on our older parent doing his or her part. That part, very simply, is being weak enough to receive our care.

It may sound odd, but if Genevieve is unwilling to be cared for, then I'm robbed of the value of the caregiving. Her power to change my life lies in how well she is willing to be weak. It is a strange paradox—what Christopher de Vinck calls "the power of the powerless."*

This doesn't mean the older person must become passive and weak in all areas. Part of the job of aging well is to recognize the difference between what he or she is able to do and what is needed from a caregiver. Successful aging doesn't mean running a marathon at age eighty; it is refusing to give up and become helpless. Show me an older person who's had a hip replacement and bad eyesight, and who walks out to the mailbox daily and uses a magnifying glass to read, and I'll show you a person who is aging successfully. An older person

---

*Christopher de Vinck, *The Power of the Powerless* (Grand Rapids: Zondervan, 1995).

must be willing to do what he or she is still able to do, even with modifications to the task. But he or she must also be willing to accept care when the task can no longer be performed.

There's one last thing an older person is required to do. The wisdom of his or her years should result in singing the praises and truth of God:

> Since my youth, O God, you have taught me,
>   and to this day I declare your marvelous deeds.
> Even when I am old and gray,
>   do not forsake me, O God,
> till I declare your power to the next generation,
>   your might to all who are to come.
>
> Psalm 71:17–18

I've seen many older parents cared for over the years. An older parent may be weak and extremely needy, but when he or she sings the praises of God, family members practically compete with one another to have the opportunity to be the caregiver. On the other hand, when the older person is mired in complaining, family members stay away in droves. This is a simple truth, but it's one that has a huge impact on caregiving.

WE'RE IN IT TOGETHER

The average caregiver is a married female in her fifties, with a full-time job. About 75 to 80 percent of married women work outside the home, yet these same women perform about 80 percent of the tasks required to keep a household running. This is conspicuously unfair and is helping to wear down one of the family's essential resources—namely, women.

Our society, especially Christian society, has trained both men and women to believe that household management and caregiving is a woman's job. Not only is this unsupported by the Bible's teaching, it is most unhealthy for the family. For a couple who have a parent or in-law in need of care, it must be a *cooperative* effort. I don't *help* take care of my mother-in-law, which implies that I assist my wife in her responsibility; *I* am responsible for giving care. If I fall into the trap of assigning caregiving to the female, I'll lose the blessing that caregiving can offer and run the risk of driving my wife to utter exhaustion and frustration.

This isn't to say there shouldn't be a lead player in the caregiving task. Indeed, caregiving works best with a lead person. But caregiving must be a team effort. I think of it like a basketball team that has a really big star. Perennial all-star Michael Jordan played with four other players at a time, but he did most of the shooting and directing of the action. Children, brothers, sisters, and friends will occasionally move in to take the ball with the older person and get him or her to a doctor's appointment or activity, but it is the Michael Jordan of the caregiving team who will do most of the direction and perform most of the activities.

LIFE ON THE ANVIL

We all treasure those moments when we don't need to do anything or be anywhere. For me, those moments occur most often in Red River, New Mexico, where my family and I retreat for a few days a year to do nothing and sleep late, and where our only concern is to find a rock that will skip eight times across the lake instead of the normal three or four.

There's nothing wrong with this relaxation, of course. It gives us time to think, refresh, and renew. But as Americans, many of us now see rest and relaxation as our *right*—that somehow our lives are strange and devalued if we don't have it. For most of the world, the fight to stay alive, provide for family members, and meet the daily obligations leaves no time for rest at all. Only in our fat and relaxed state do we begin to think we have the good life. Most of us expect our life to be just the way we want it to be, and somehow we believe it's the way we *deserve* it to be.

The Bible reveals just the opposite. Life is not an end in itself but rather a means by which we learn, most often through relationship. In other words, life is life. There is time for retreat, but it's a time to be used for focus and refreshment before we once again take up the enormous tasks of life. It is a privilege, not a right. The Bible suggests that it is in the angst of life that the real story will be told of who we are and who God is. In our time, the task of caring amid the vast business of our lives puts us on the anvil, where God sharpens us and reshapes us so we can become more and more like him.

If the twentieth century was the age of medicine, which extended the human life span to new heights, then the twenty-first century will be the age of older living and caregiving. Caregivers will have to recognize the requirements of older people, evaluate the available resources and services, and somehow learn to balance the principles of responsibility, openhandedness, and evenness. How we cope with the challenges and make the necessary adaptations will show our mettle, mold our characters, and shape our souls.

Questions for Consideration

1. What hopes and dreams did you have for your personal life and family before you took on the job of caregiving?

2. In what ways do you hold yourself responsible for caregiving that may be unhealthy for you and bad for your family?

3. What practical things can you do that would help you balance your caregiving job with the responsibilities you carry for your family and community?

4

When Physical Things
Can't Be Fixed

Strengthen the feeble hands,
  steady the knees that give way;
say to those with fearful hearts,
  "Be strong, do not fear;
your God will come,
  he will come with vengeance;
with divine retribution
  he will come to save you."
Isaiah 35:3–4

Some disasters in history seem so cruel or ironic that we wait for someone to pop in and say, "Just kidding." Such must have been the case for the passengers aboard the *Titanic*.

The beautiful *Titanic* was the epitome of everything modern, technological, and powerful. Many boasted she was unsinkable. Everything about the ship spoke of the best that humankind had to offer. Yet on her first voyage across the Atlantic, the ship struck an iceberg and broke apart before sinking beneath miles of water. Imagine the disbelief of passengers as they stood on the decks of the mighty liner, hearing whispers of concern here and there. Imagine how they must have shaken their heads as they waited for their space on a lifeboat. Imagine their utter shock as the crippled behemoth broke apart and sank. It couldn't be true. It simply had to be a joke.

Many Americans look at their lives in much the same way. As a society, we live longer, healthier lives—with more resources at our fingertips than ever before. It's easy to act as though we will live forever, simply because we do not often have to face death. Somewhere in our subconscious we know we age, but the thought gets left out of our conversations or comes up only in the context of a joke or a funny birthday card.

Yet anyone over forty can tell you that aging is no joke. It may be we just don't have the stamina we used to. It may be our joints now predict an upcoming change in the weather. Or it just may be our natural hair color can't be found in a beginner set of watercolors. Whatever we say or deny about aging, it marches on and will have its way with our bodies. As we have learned how to extend the human life span, aging simply provides more time to wear out more parts. Therefore, caregivers have to be aware of the physical toll of aging, how to accurately assess the implications of such wear, and how to find the solutions or adaptations that can address the practical physical problems aging brings.

WHAT HAPPENS WHEN WE AGE?

In the technical sense, researchers refer to aging as a change process that (1) lowers our probability of survival, (2) decreases our ability to take care of ourselves, (3) lowers our ability to heal physically, and (4) decreases our ability to meet the challenges our environment presents. Aging is part of the consequence of sin, which in the end returns us to dust:

By the sweat of your brow
 you will eat your food
until you return to the ground,
  since from it you were taken;
for dust you are
 and to dust you will return.
Genesis 3:19

How did God put aging into the mix? Two theories circulate. One says we are genetically built to start self-destructing. Aging presents itself at a programmed time of life, just like puberty occurs around early adolescence. The second maintains that the events of life, the environment, and the elements simply wear us down and out until things stop working—similar to piling up too many miles on the car. Both theories have elements of truth.

While all of us age in different ways and at different rates, it's helpful to get a general idea of the biological deterioration that comes with aging.

Sensory Perception

Everything we know about our surroundings comes to us through the windows of our sensations: touching, tasting, seeing, hearing, smelling. Aging affects every sensation in our bodies so that we have to receive greater stimulation from the environment to achieve the same impact as when we were younger. In order to see as well as we did at age twenty, we need the objects to be closer, with more light surrounding them.

Of all the sensory declines we suffer during aging, none is more pronounced than vision reduction. More than half of all cases of blindness develop in people over the age of sixty-five. The sharpness of vision and the adaptation to light fall off more and more with age, which challenges our abilities to read, work, drive, and manage household functions. As we age, we become more and more at risk of developing cataracts, glaucoma, macular degeneration, or vision loss due to diabetes.

Of those over age sixty-five, half will have significant hearing loss; the problem is more pronounced in men than women. Hearing loss is particularly difficult because as we lose our ability to interpret and understand communication, we get frustrated and tend to withdraw from social situations and even our relationships.

Taste buds in the mouth and nerve fibers in the nose also lose density as we age, resulting in a reduction in abilities to taste and smell. Many older people complain more about food or tend to spice their food more as they age, because it simply "doesn't taste the way it should."

Cardiovascular System

We depend on oxygen-rich blood getting pumped to every part of our bodies. Our hearts pump that blood. Television ads promoting antiaging formulas often mention collagen—a fibrous connective tissue that essentially holds all of our muscles and organs together. As we age, our collagen loses its elasticity, and we begin losing flexibility in every part of our bodies. This is especially a problem when it comes to the cardiovascular system. As fat gets deposited on the heart's surface, the collagen surrounding the heart stiffens, requiring the heart to work harder to pump blood. As the fat deposits grow and the heart loses muscle bulk, the amount of blood pumped to the rest of the body decreases and oxygen levels in the blood drop. Our arterial walls stiffen with changes in the collagen, making it more likely that fat deposits will form in our arteries. In short, as we age, our risk for heart attacks and strokes increases. Plus, the reduction of oxygen-rich blood to the brain, organs, and our extremities contribute to a variety of health problems and complications.

Although some older people function just fine with only slight reductions in blood flow, some significant factors can greatly complicate cardiovascular risk. This first is high blood pressure, which puts arterial walls at risk and stresses the heart muscle. Losing weight, watching diet, and lowering salt intake can lower blood pressure, but a few very effective medications can also make treatment successful. High cholesterol is another problem. Simply stated, cholesterol is a fatlike substance that sticks to the wall of blood vessels. It increases the risk of high blood pressure and stroke and can make it difficult for the heart to function properly.

Other key factors include angina and congestive heart failure. Angina is a type of chest pain that occurs when the heart cannot get the oxygen it needs; it's often due to blockage of a major artery. The blockage can be treated by medication, arterial interventions such as angioplasty or placement of stents, or coronary artery bypass surgery. Congestive heart failure damages the heart either through age or oxygen deprivation, resulting in a reduction of pumping capacity. This, in turn, results in blood backing up into the major organs and a buildup of fluid in all the tissues. Congestive heart failure cannot be reversed but can be slowed significantly with proper medication.

Respiratory System

Loss of elasticity in the collagen can cause big problems for the respiratory system. As we lose flexibility and elasticity in our rib cages, we have a lower capacity for inhaling and exhaling. As muscles weaken throughout the body, a weak diaphragm and poor posture contribute to lower lung capacity. Not only does this have a direct effect on the oxygen supply in the blood; it also accounts for higher incidences of emphysema, bronchitis, and pneumonia.

Musculoskeletal System

This system consists of the muscles and bones that help us move and carry out both demanding athletic tasks and simple everyday tasks like brushing our teeth. We used to think people's muscles naturally weakened with age; now we know people can maintain a good part of their strength as long as they exercise vigorously. Older people lose much of their muscle strength when they get less active. The adage "use it or lose it" is genuinely true.

Some minor changes occur in our height as we age due to gravity compressing our spinal cords or to poor posture, but most of the skeletal changes occur in the structure of our bones. As we grow older, our bones become less dense and more porous, which makes us more susceptible to fractures. Older women are particularly vulnerable to the loss of calcium in their bones, which may lead to osteoporosis. Common problems like back pain and arthritis make it difficult for older people to do basic tasks like cooking and cleaning, or even some hygiene tasks like bathing.

Nervous System

Here we're mostly concerned with the central nervous system—the brain and spinal column. All movement, speech, thought, and emotion originate in and are carried out from the brain and spinal column through a complex network of special cells called neurons. Billions of these neurons communicate with one another and pass along messages through an electrochemical process. A healthy brain has many big, robust neurons capable of passing along messages to other neurons—like a dense tree root system.

With all the advances in medical science over the past hundred years, the brain and nervous system remain the most mysterious aspects of the human body. Tremendous research efforts over the past decade, however, have yielded a treasure trove of knowledge that is sure to grow over the next decade.

Consider some of the things we've learned: As we age, the overall weight of the brain decreases, which may be due to decreased blood flow. The number of neurons in certain regions of the brain also decreases. The frontal lobe, the part responsible for complex thought processes (like planning, language, or performing artistic functions), is most at risk for losing these neurons. In addition, neurons tend to shrink, and the structures responsible for passing along messages tend to decrease. Finally, the neurons in the older brain don't appear to be as active.

At a minimum, this means our brains don't retain or exchange as much information between neurons as they did when we were younger. Strokes, Parkinson's disease, and Alzheimer's disease are some of the more common nervous system disorders associated with aging. Strokes are a leading cause of death among older people and result from a reduction or cutoff of blood supply to certain areas of the brain. Survivors of strokes may be left with a physical or mental impairment. Parkinson's primarily affects motor activity, while Alzheimer's affects memory, orientation, emotional stability, and thinking.

For most older people who haven't been affected by stroke or disease, changes in the nervous system have a minimal effect on life. Reaction time and brain activity may slow, but not in such a way that it affects the individual's ability to function in normal, everyday life. Memory does decline but not necessarily in a profound way. A number of well-researched studies indicate that if we use our brains through vigorous cognitive activity—such as reading, playing games, and interacting in conversation—we can stave off memory loss and even reduce our chances of getting Alzheimer's disease. Again the adage holds true: "Use it or lose it!"

Psychological Changes

When I first began my work in the personal care facility, I visited Alicia, one of my new residents. Eighty-six-year-old Alicia was not happy about moving into the home. In my effort to connect, I said, "Well, Alicia, how does it feel to be eighty-six?"

Angrily she narrowed her eyelids at me and asked, "How old are you?"

At the time I was thirty-two, so I told her so. She volleyed back, "Well, how does it feel to be thirty-two?"

I thought for a moment and responded, "I guess it feels like I am me."

"Well, that's how it feels to be eighty-six," she snapped. "It feels like me."

We sometimes think aging somehow disconnects us from the personalities we knew at a younger age—but it doesn't. Alicia is correct. We remain who we were when we were younger. Our personalities don't change so much as our focus does. When we are young, we tend to look to the future. What will we do when our children graduate from school? Where we will take our next vacation? How can we improve our marketability in our job or profession? But as we age, we realize we have many more years behind us than in front of us. Most older people, especially those who have suffered a major illness or trauma, begin to evaluate their lives—what they have done in the past. If they have lived well, they have a sense of wisdom and accomplishment; if they have not lived up to their values or aspirations—especially in relationships—they cannot go back and change things, and they sense they lack the time to make things different. These older people often tend to feel hopeless or depressed.

Many older people deal with multiple relationship losses, including the loss of spouses and friends, as well as losses of job roles, homes, or status. Depression in the aging population is a special risk—one we'll discuss in depth in chapter 9. But not all older people get discouraged as they confront these losses. Most will negotiate the task well and remain vital and emotionally connected with family members and friends.

ASSESSING THE CAREGIVING NEED

All of us age, and as we do most of us will have at least some of the problems mentioned above. But these problems don't affect all of us in the same way. One older person with arthritis, for instance, may not be able to cook at all, while another cooks big Thanksgiving dinners. When impairments start to afflict older people, it's necessary to take a good look at the *gravity* of impairment.

It takes sober thinking and careful communication in order to address and make it through the hard situations of life. In working with families during a crisis, it always amazes me that, at just the time a family needs the clearest thinking and the greatest communication, many choose to ignore the obvious. It's as though they believe that denial will make the problem go away; the problem will have no power unless they mention it to one another. Many try this approach when their older parents start deteriorating and then never quite catch up to caregiving at an appropriate level.

Denial is a great enemy. Most of the problems of aging cannot be fixed, and because of that, we must assess needs properly to determine a necessary level of care.

The Alphabet of Assessment

The elder care service industry uses Instrumental Activities of Daily Living (IADLs) and Activities of Daily Living (ADLs) to assess an older person's ability to function. IADLs assess several basic activities required to maintain independent living, such as doing housekeeping and laundry, cooking meals, driving, planning, paying bills, and knowing what medications need to be taken and when. ADLs are not associated with independent living as much as with independent function, and they include things like the ability to eat without assistance, bathing, dressing, toileting, brushing teeth, getting up and around without assistance, and the ability to take medications without assistance.

In both IADLs and ADLs, we watch to see how the older person is doing with nutrition, planning/managing, mobility, medication, and hygiene. Unless your parent or older person has some catastrophic or sudden downturn—which is true, for instance, after a stroke or a fractured hip—most often we'll see deterioration in the IADLs before we'll see problems in the ADLs. In other words, the older person will have difficulty maintaining independent living before he or she has difficulty maintaining independent function.

We knew for some time that my mother-in-law, Genevieve, was deteriorating cognitively—possibly due to her chronic drinking or to the early stages of Alzheimer's. We began to notice she was having difficulty cooking meals regularly, was unable or unwilling to purchase even basic clothing items, and was failing to clean her apartment. All these things began threatening her ability to live independently, even though she was able to eat, bathe, and get around by herself. Once this process of deterioration started in earnest, Genevieve stayed in her apartment, but we began having to "plug the holes" to maintain her independent living. They weren't big things— we cooked three meals a week and delivered them to her; Sharon went shopping for her and restocked her clothes; we'd clean her apartment when she was out—but they were signals of the beginning of the caregiving task. As happens with many caregivers, once we started the process of plugging a few holes, more holes soon started appearing.

The first major gap in Genevieve's ability to maintain her independent living occurred when she developed a severe sinus infection but refused to go to the doctor. She finally called Sharon to take her in, and while at the doctor's office, she suffered a mild stroke. She was hospitalized for several days for tests. Sharon's brother, John, came for a week to help us evaluate how she would score on both the IADLs and the ADLs. Although it wasn't a "slam dunk," enough of Genevieve's IADLs had deteriorated to the point we all knew she would require permanent meal and transportation assistance.

After it became clear we had taken on a caregiving role, we became more aggressive in evaluating whether some of Genevieve's problems could be treated medically. For instance, would taking medication improve her memory? Would keeping her off alcohol improve her ability to maintain her apartment or help her be more willing to purchase clothes? Sometimes these things can be improved dramatically for several years—and sometimes they can't—but it's certainly worth the effort if an aging person's independence can be restored.

More and more of Genevieve's IADLs began to decline. Soon she couldn't keep track of her finances or medications; nor could she perform any housekeeping chores. Around this time we started seeing a clear deterioration in her ADLs. Genevieve was unable or unwilling to bathe herself. She soon needed assistance with dressing appropriately. The time was coming when she would need help with virtually all her ADLs, including feeding herself.

Properly assessing Genevieve's abilities helped us plan more precisely the kind of caregiving she required. Below is an adapted chart you can use to assess your older parent's ability to maintain independent living or functioning:

Area	Function or Task	Able to Perform Task Reasonably Well	Has Difficulty Performing the Task Regularly	Caregiving Required to Accomplish the Task
Nutrition *Instrumental ADLs*	Planning appropriate meals Cooking meals safely	☐ ☐	☐ ☐	☐ ☐
ADLs	Knowing when to eat Feeding oneself	☐ ☐	☐ ☐	☐ ☐
Mobility *Instrumental ADLs*	Able to drive or take a bus Doing grocery shopping Capable of doing errands	☐ ☐ ☐	☐ ☐ ☐	☐ ☐ ☐
ADLs	Unassisted walking Transferring from chairs 　or bed unassisted	☐ ☐	☐ ☐	☐ ☐
Medications *Instrumental ADLs*	Knowing medication regimen Reordering medications	☐ ☐	☐ ☐	☐ ☐
ADLs	Able to take medications unassisted	☐	☐	☐
Managing *Instrumental ADLs*	Unassisted housekeeping Managing finances Using telephone	☐ ☐ ☐	☐ ☐ ☐	☐ ☐ ☐
ADLs	Oriented to time and place Appropriate behavior 　in social situations	☐ ☐	☐ ☐	☐ ☐
Hygiene *Instrumental ADLs*	Taking care of laundry	☐	☐	☐
ADLs	Bathing/showering Unassisted toileting Dressing Brushing teeth	☐ ☐ ☐ ☐	☐ ☐ ☐ ☐	☐ ☐ ☐ ☐

How Will the Older Person Accept Caregiving?

From doing the assessment of IADLs and ADLs, it may become clear that the older person needs care. Older people tend to adapt to caregiving in four basic ways. These methods of adaptation will greatly affect how the older person accepts caregiving and works with you.

The "Make Lemonade" Type

Dorothy was ninety-eight when I first met her. Her husband had died thirty-two years before, and her only son was struggling with cancer. She came to our personal care home with a bad case of shingles, which was making her physically miserable. From my perspective, she had every right to be angry, depressed, unpleasant, and unhappy.

To the contrary, Dorothy was appreciative and kind to every person charged with her care. If an aide said it was time to treat her sores, she cooperated. If it was time to go to a meal, she tried to make pleasant conversation. When I visited her to suggest that a walk would do her some good, she said, "You know, I don't walk very well. But if you're willing to pick me up if I fall, I'll give it a try."

Dorothy was what I call a "Make Lemonade" person, as in, "If life hands you lemons, make lemonade." These older people will accept their limitations as a part of life and will do their best to adapt to the requirements laid in front of them. If they need caregiving, they'll almost always work with the caregiver to keep functioning at a maximum level. These folks present no problems when it comes time for caregiving. They will not only accept it, but they'll usually make the job as pleasant as possible.

The "Pretend It's Not Happening" Type

Some older people exhibit a tenacious desire to keep functioning. If they have no profound needs, they manage pretty well to keep the ball of daily tasks moving in the right direction. But when they start having more needs than they can handle by themselves, they often resist accepting any kind of caregiving. Instead, they prefer to try to make their lives work, which can result in the situation getting worse or dangerous—and certainly unpleasant.

Josie was only sixty-nine, but she had had a colostomy when she was sixty-seven and had deteriorated significantly. She had difficulty walking, got confused about her medications, was unable to cook for herself, and could not change her colostomy bag. Her son initially tried to drop by her house every day after work to make sure she had eaten and taken her meds and to help her with any tasks. More often than not he'd find she hadn't eaten, taken her meds, or gotten dressed, and she had made a terrible mess in the bathroom. He would spend the next two hours getting things squared away. You would think Josie would have felt grateful. Not so. Josie would follow him around, cursing at him and telling him she could take care of herself and he should leave.

Her son tried to hire a home care agency to help his mother five days a week. Josie would lock the door and not allow the worker in. "I don't know why you're here. I don't need any help!" she would shout. Her son then moved Josie to our personal care facility, hoping we could provide the care she needed. We discovered that every moment we provided care for Josie, she was prone to attack us verbally and insist she didn't need our help.

Why was Josie being so difficult? Why couldn't she adapt to her needs? Why did she fight the reality of her needs every step of the way? She was a "Pretend It's Not Happening" person.

If your older parent is of this type, you may feel as though you're beating your head against a brick wall. No wonder many caregivers of these older people say things like, "Fine! You don't want my help, I won't offer it! Let's see how you make it by yourself!" Of course, this withdrawal makes the situation worse, and often the older parent then turns and gets angry at the adult child for being irresponsible and neglectful. If you deal with an older person of this type, you often feel in a double bind—you lose if you try to help; you lose if you don't help.

If you are a caregiver for this kind of person, you'll have to steel yourself to staying in the game and doing what is right. You know your older person needs care, so you set your jaw and keep giving the necessary care, come what may. If the older person doesn't cooperate or responds with meanness, you simply keep on offering the care and setting a boundary of not letting them speak to you in a particular manner. In other words, you become a battering ram to the person's defensive posture and behavior.

When we had to deal with Josie on changing her colostomy bag, for instance, we'd go to her room and engage her in small talk for a few minutes. We'd then say something like, "I know you don't like me to help change your bag, but it's something that has to be done. I can't leave until we get it accomplished, so we can make it difficult or easy." Then my staff or I would keep talking and dominate the conversation so Josie would have little or no opportunity to complain or toss out accusations. We weren't setting this boundary to be mean, of course, but to keep us from getting caught in the crazy conversation that would otherwise ensue.

Older people are fully adult. Even if they need care, they still have charge of their own bodies. We don't have the right to *make* them do anything, anymore than we have the right to make any adult do anything. But as people charged with caregiving, our most powerful tool is that we do not go away.

We would not make Josie change her bag, but we made it clear we wouldn't move on until we got the work accomplished. At first, she grumbled and was argumentative for about twenty to thirty minutes. We would just listen to music, pausing every now and again to tell her we weren't going to leave until the job was finished. Eventually she'd consent. The more we hung in there, the shorter the time it took to get her bag changed.

The "Poor Pitiful Me" Type

The opposite of the "Pretend It's Not Happening" person is the "Poor Pitiful Me" person. This kind of person doesn't resist caregiving; instead, he wants the caregiver to envelope him, and thus he becomes helpless to do anything.

Elizabeth called me about her sixty-eight-year-old mother, Elsie. "Mom is driving me crazy," she said. "She calls me to say she can't stand up. Yet when I go over and give her the least bit of assistance, she stands right up. She'll tell me she can't keep her medications straight, so I put them in a weekly medication box. Then she calls and says she needs me to come over and show her what pills to take. It's driving me up the wall, and I really think she can do some of these things for herself."

It is indeed difficult to provide the appropriate care for an older parent who sees it as your full-time job. Most "Poor Pitiful Me" people manipulate their caregivers because they fear something. I usually find they feel anxious about their own competence, the idea of their own death, or the impending death of someone close to them. The more anxious they become, the more they handle the anxiety by asking for help. As a caregiver becomes annoyed or comes to the end of his or her rope, the older person then becomes anxious that the caregiver will quit, which in turn can make him or her that much more manipulative.

When I spoke with Elsie, I found out quickly that her anxiety flowed from her fear of death. Elsie anxiously said, "My mother died when she was sixty-eight, and I just get afraid I'll have something that my mother had. I know I will be in heaven, but I just get so scared and want someone to calm me down."

When someone feels this anxious, usually they've carried anxiety around all their lives. So I asked Elsie, "How did you handle your fears when you were younger?"

"I just was so busy I didn't have the time to worry," she said.

Next I spoke to Elsie about what she did in her younger years. She had run a very tight household and worked part-time as a reporter for the town's weekly newspaper. In her day, she had gotten a bead on everything happening in her community.

In order to help Elizabeth get a feel for the proper amount of care her mother required, we did a review of the IADLs and ADLs and determined that her mother did need help with doing the shopping, paying bills, getting around town, and getting her weekly medications placed in a medication box, but Elsie could do just about everything else. I met with both of them and outlined for Elsie what Elizabeth was prepared to do in her job as caregiver, and then I added, "I'm going to suggest she do nothing else but these things. But you have a job to do also. I want you to keep up on what's going on in town. Elizabeth will ask you about that every time you call, and if you can't tell her anything, she'll have to call a halt to the conversation."

"But I need Elizabeth," Elsie objected.

"I know you need her for some help," I responded, "but you must be willing to do your work also." I gently reminded her of a couple of Bible verses: "We hear that some among you are idle. They are not busy; they are busybodies. Such people we command and urge in the Lord Jesus Christ to settle down and earn the bread they eat" (2 Thessalonians 3:11–12).

I instructed Elizabeth to resist doing for Elsie what she could do for herself. I told her, "You must say something like, 'I believe you can do that for yourself, Mother.'" I then told her she must ask what was going on in town every time her mother called. This strategy was important, because it changed Elsie's focus and helped her cope with her anxiety. Finally, I told Elizabeth she'd have to get an answering machine with caller identification. If her mother did not pick up any town news, Elizabeth was to let the answering machine take her mother's calls for the rest of the day.

Of course, this personality type will push the boundary. Elizabeth had to consistently not do for Elsie what she could do for herself. At first, Elsie would ring Elizabeth's phone off the wall some days. But making calls to find out what was going on in town calmed Elsie's anxiety. As Elizabeth stuck to the boundary, Elsie did more of the investigatory work I had assigned and also became more competent at home. As the caregiving issue became clearer, it opened the way for me to do some therapeutic work with Elsie regarding her anxiety.

I have one final warning for those who provide care for this type of person. Once you set your focus on the caregiving tasks that should be performed, you must be willing to stick to those tasks alone. It'll mean that many tasks will go undone. If you pick up these tasks that should be done by the elderly person, then his or her manipulation has worked. You must remain stalwart and do *only* the necessary caregiving, or your older parent will become dependent long before he or she should.

The "Whatever" Type

Aging is tough, and it is part of a process of the body becoming disabled and moving down the road to eventual death. With some older people, this process takes place very quickly, and they may feel like giving in or giving up. Perhaps the older person simply acknowledges the aging and thinks he must let it have its way, or maybe she feels hopeless or depressed about the future and cannot muster the energy to try to cope with the realities of each day.

This type of older person often accepts caregiving with little problem, not because he or she is trying to adapt, but because he or she is passive. It's important with the "Whatever" person to recognize the problems of depression discussed in chapter 9 but also to connect with the older person in relationship. It's often helpful to spend time not only in caregiving but also in helping them look back at life—perhaps through a developmental review of his or her life.

Although you may not have firsthand knowledge of all the events of your parent's lifetime, you do know something about the major events of history. The major events of the twentieth century are such things as World War I, the Great Depression, World War II, the Cold War, the assassination of John Kennedy, astronauts walking on the moon, and the Vietnam conflict. While many of us have a bird's-eye view of these events from history books, the elderly person has a worm's-eye view of how these events actually transpired in her or his experience.

An eighty-year-old man, for example, was a child in the Great Depression, may well have served in the armed forces during World War II, was married and raised children through the Cold War, and nurtured teens during the Vietnam conflict and the upheaval of the 1960s. You'll find a wealth of story there if you only take the time to ask and connect as you affirm the person's life experiences and perspective. This connection is a great experience for both you and the older person, but most important, it helps the passive older person become more integrated into the present.

Aging Trajectory

There's one last issue to consider in assessing the caregiving to be provided. Once your older parent begins to need care, the caregiving duties likely will only increase. *How* they will increase, however, greatly affects how you plan for the future.

One trajectory involves *gradual decline*. For example, my mother-in-law, Genevieve, is in otherwise good health, except for Alzheimer's disease. This disease tends to work slowly on the brain, and we usually can plan on the older person requiring more and more caregiving over a three- to ten-year period until the disease finally kills the person. After Genevieve's memory started faltering and she stopped taking proper care of herself, I could accurately estimate she would be dependent in two years, because the trajectory of her disease is fairly predictable. When an older person is on such a gradual decline, you make plans that keep you one step ahead. For instance, when Genevieve moved into an apartment complex that provided transportation and meals, we began planning to take over her finances and investigated personal care facilities.

Another aging trajectory is *dramatic decline*. This kind of decline occurs most often in an older person with an injury or disease, and it requires rapid changes in caregiving. For instance, Tom was seventy-three when he developed Parkinson's disease. Because of Tom's age, the disease progressed rapidly, and he lost a significant portion of his motor control within eight months. By that time, he had to be fed at every meal and needed to be helped everywhere he went. In such cases, caregivers must develop a total care plan that can be put into effect quickly. Tom's daughter took a week off from work to interview home care workers who could stay with Tom, investigated care facilities that could care for her father full-time, and reviewed a full treatment plan with Tom's neurologist. She did not put all of this caregiving plan into effect immediately, but it was ready when Tom declined quickly.

Finally, there is an *erratic trajectory*. In these types of declines, drops in function occur sometimes in a gradual way and at other times in dramatic fashion. In these cases, the caregiving preparation has to be undertaken two or three steps ahead of where the older person currently needs it. For instance, Jerry was seventy-one and had diabetes. He was stable but also very fragile. We had to keep a close eye on him because, like many older diabetics, his poor circulation was endangering his left leg. Jerry's family not only had to have a plan for the next place Jerry would stay if he needed a higher level of care; they had to have a medical caregiving plan if Jerry lost a leg.

Knowing the needs of your older person, assessing how he or she could adapt to the caregiving process, and investigating the likely future caregiving requirements should give you a sense of how to proceed with the caregiving task. If you do the necessary assessment and planning, you'll be facing the challenges of aging head-on.

THREE SPECIAL ISSUES THAT NEED ADDRESSING

As we age, three uniquely important issues need to be carefully and sensitively addressed. They all can cause big problems if we fail to give them the attention they deserve.

Medications

"My mother can't walk anymore," Dan said. "I don't understand it; she was fine a month ago, but now she's simply out of it more and more. I thought I would be a caregiver; I just didn't think it would come on like this."

When I see an older person in need of care, I ask to see either a list of medications or the actual medication bottles. When I saw Dan's mother and father, they brought along a container of Valium. I asked what the pills were for.

"Oh, the doctor said these are for when she gets nervous," her husband replied. "I give her one whenever she's nervous."

"How nervous has she been lately?" I said.

"All the time."

Dan's mother wasn't crippled; she simply was so stoned she couldn't walk.

As a general rule, the older people get, the more medications they take. Therefore, the risk of drug misuse increases with age. Three problems plague the public with regard to medications, but especially plague the aging population: harmful drug interactions, inability to follow prescription directions, and confusion in taking medications intended for others.

Older people have a variety of physical problems and complaints. In our society, medicine has become a very specialized field, and so there's a good chance your older parent will have several doctors. Each doctor must see a list of current prescriptions and dosages. Don't assume doctors communicate with one another about a patient's medications. It's up to you to be the advocate and communicator between doctors.

When a doctor prescribes a new medication, you as the caregiver should ask exactly what the medication is for, how long it's prescribed for, what the possible side effects are, and what the possible interactions are with other drugs your older parent is taking. When a prescription gets filled, it's also wise to speak with the pharmacist about possible drug interactions. On return visits to doctors, you should not hesitate to ask whether current medications are still necessary.

Older people tend to vary wildly on how to handle prescription drugs. Many reason, "If one pill makes me feel a little better, then two pills will make me feel a lot better." In the same way, they figure, "If that pill works for you, then it should work for me in the same way." But medications can't work properly unless they are taken as prescribed—in fact, they can have dangerous side effects or interactions. It's usually best to keep only those medications in the household that are currently in use—and this holds true for nonprescription medications like cold medications or aspirin as well. You or another caregiver can also prepare weekly medication boxes that contain only the number of pills for a particular day. Stress to the older person that the medications are to be taken *only* as prescribed. If he or she is unable to keep the medications straight or take them properly, it's time for the medication regimen to be overseen directly by you or another care provider.

Incontinence

Incontinence is a major issue in aging and caregiving. It eventually affects more than half of the elderly population in nursing homes and occurs mostly in women.

Incontinence has several causes. First, the muscles that support the bladder may have been damaged through the years by childbirth or hormonal changes. Sudden movement, hard laughter, or coughing may result in urination. Second, the primary muscle that controls urinary flow loses its ability to control the flow, and a small but constant leak results. Third, there may not be enough control between the time the urge is felt until the time urination begins.

Although incontinence is embarrassing, there's seldom any real effort to solve the problem except through the wearing of adult incontinence protection. These types of briefs are extremely helpful, and there should be no hesitation in using them. But several other things can also help solve incontinence: (1) make sure the older person isn't taking medications that may result in incontinence; (2) try to schedule regular bathroom breaks, even if he or she doesn't feel a strong urge to urinate; (3) avoid intake of items that make continence more difficult, such as caffeine, sugar, and spicy food; (4) be careful about the intake of liquids one to three hours before bedtime; and (5) make access to the bathroom easy by keeping a clear path from room to room.

Driving

For those who live in places that have limited or no public transportation, automobiles are one of the most important symbols of independence. I can go where I want to go when I want to go, and I can determine how fast I want to go. I am in control. But there's also a practical side to driving. If I can drive, I can get the groceries I need and the socialization I want, and I can get myself to the places where I need to be, such as work and appointments.

When an older person starts declining physically, it's hard to decide when he or she should give up driving. On the one hand, if he or she stops driving, an immediate requirement for stepped-up transportation assistance occurs, whether through taxis, community assistance, or (which is most often the case) friends or family members doing the driving. On the other hand, a decline in the older person's reaction times, depth perception, vision, and general awareness may present a hazard on the road to oneself and others. And yet there remains the desire for control. In many ways, driving represents independence and security for older people. There's no easy answer for determining the time to give up the car keys.

Eighty-one-year-old Cynthia had always been perfectly competent as a driver. But when she started having difficulty with her eyesight, her daughter, Jessica, tried to get her to stop driving. Cynthia was enraged at the suggestion, and it became such an issue that she threatened to stop speaking to her daughter. Jessica contacted me to see if I could help. After asking Cynthia some general questions about her life, I asked about her driving.

"I've been driving since I was sixteen and never had one accident," she said. "Maybe I don't see as well, but I can drive just fine."

I asked her to go outside with me to see what objects she could see and where she had problems. Her daughter was right; her vision had deteriorated enough that it felt a little scary to think she was still driving. I decided to ask Cynthia, "Where do you drive now?"

"Only to the grocery store and to church on Sunday," she replied.

After inquiring about the location of the store, I asked Jessica to ride as a passenger with her mother to these places. "I want you to ride with her to the store and church and evaluate if she's safe. Be sure not to evaluate whether she drives like you. Many older people actually drive slower and safer because they know they have limited vision and reaction times."

Jessica and Cynthia came back the following week, and Jessica reported, "You were right. She doesn't drive like I do, but she did nothing unsafe. But on her way to church, she has to cross two busy streets. I wish she'd let me drive her to church."

I asked Cynthia if she'd be willing to let her daughter drive her to church if she could keep driving to the store. Cynthia hesitated but finally agreed to make the compromise. She drove for another two years until she fell and broke her arm. At that point, she had adjusted enough to riding with her daughter she was able to give up driving completely.

While it's a tough issue, caregivers must be especially sensitive and not just assume they have the right to take away the car keys. Carefully consider the emotional implications, as well as the safety concerns. Be willing to start providing alternate transportation for the older person before they have to give up driving completely. Finally, be sure you evaluate the older person's driving fairly—don't just base it on your own driving preference.

A good and impartial way to evaluate driving is to contact your Department of Public Safety. Once notified regarding a change in a person's health, this agency usually has the authority to require a driver to come in for a driving test. By doing so, you'll take the decision-making process (and possibly the battle) out of the relationship and put it in the court of a neutral party that has the training and knowledge necessary to make a clear judgment.

KNOW WHEN TO TAKE THE PLATES DOWN

Perhaps you feel a bit overwhelmed after having read this chapter. Physical decline and health issues of an older parent are complicated. It's confusing to try to get a handle on all the assessment necessary to make good caregiving decisions. Knowing when and where caregiving help for an older parent will be effective and when it could make your parent more dependent and less competent demands the wisdom of Solomon. The fact is that the ins and outs of caregiving *are* overwhelming. How do we do it all?

I have a dear friend from my college days who is extremely talented at juggling and entertaining. One of the "tricks" of his act is spinning a number of plates on poles and keeping them all up in the air for several minutes—first four plates, then eight, then ten, and on it goes. Amazed at his ability, I asked him his secret. He shot off a quick answer: "Keep moving." As I chuckled, he added, "And know when to take the plates down."

Caregiving will stretch us toward growth in many ways, but the task is almost always accompanied by stress. We work and try to succeed at a situation that gets more complicated by the month. At times it feels as though we are the plate spinner with only two choices: either to keep running or to let the whole job fall and get smashed to pieces.

It's important to remember that, while God does call us to the job of caregiving, the call isn't to always succeed. We make mistakes, and the older persons for whom we care will make mistakes. We are limited in our ability to keep going physically and in possessing the wisdom to interpret situations correctly. I believe God does call us to "keep moving" and to do the best job we know how to do—within our limitations. But I also believe God knows we cannot keep all those caregiving plates spinning perfectly. Sometimes we will know when it's time to "take the plate down"—and some will inevitably fall. But we must give ourselves the grace to make errors in this difficult job and not expect that we'll be 100 percent successful. We should extend this grace to ourselves because God surely does so on our behalf.

QUESTIONS FOR CONSIDERATION

1. What current limitations exist with the older person under your care?

2. How can you effectively take over the caregiving task, considering the method of adaptation of the older person in your care?

3. What most frightens you about the caregiving task? How can you get encouragement to be courageous in the task?

5

Our House Is a Very, Very,
Very Confusing Place

Lord, you have been our dwelling place
throughout all generations.
Psalm 90:1

Early in our marriage, Sharon and I had very different philoso-
phies on taking a trip. I was raised in a family in which we
would pile into a car on a moment's notice and strike out on
the open road. Sometimes we didn't know exactly where we
were going, but almost never did we have an idea where we
would stay. Whenever we got tired or saw something interesting, we would stop and try to secure lodging. If we could find
none, we resorted to our mobile holiday inn and slept in the
car. Reservations? You'd think we didn't even know the word.

Sharon, on the other hand, came from a family that metic-
ulously planned its vacations. They would consider trips a year
or two in advance, lay out routes, calculate estimated times of
arrival, and certainly *always* make reservations.

When Sharon and I traveled, it was an interesting—and
loud—experience for the first few years of our marriage. But
after twenty-five years together, we've worked out a nice way
of doing things. We plan enough in advance so we don't have

to worry about the basics but leave enough freedom in the schedule to take some chances and go on some surprising side trips.

When older parents require caregiving, it is a lot like going on a trip. The journey is likely to take both caregiver and older person through tough and rocky roads, mixed with beautiful and precious experiences. It begins with a real need and ends when the older parent dies. It is a trip to the bountiful end. But just as Sharon and I discovered on our own journey, compromise and balance must be achieved. You cannot plan out every contingency of the caregiving experience or be perfectly prepared for whatever happens; caregiving for an older parent is much too fluid and unpredictable for that. You cannot know exactly where you'll be staying and when. Because caregiving is so fluid and unpredictable, it can also threaten your livelihood, your financial security, and your health. In short, caregiving can contain an element of danger. It's wise to consider the possibilities, come up with different strategies, and make contingency plans. Be secure in knowing the general direction you and your older parent will head on the trip, but remain willing to toss the plans out the window to accommodate a few surprises along the way.

One big issue of balance in making such plans involves where your older parent will stay. You will find challenges with determining what place seems safe, the financial cost involved, and what feels emotionally tolerable to you and your parent. Few issues are as emotionally charged as "home," especially when you as a caregiver start edging into the older person's space. The issue begs for sound information on available options, clear evaluation of needs, and sensitivity to the emotional well-being of both family and older person. All of these issues came into play one day when an older woman and her sons came to see me.

LIKE STEALING A WATERMELON

An eighty-three-year-old woman named Dorothy sat in my office, waving her hands in wild gestures, barking angry accusations at her two sons, and threatening to end the relationship with her family forever. Her two sons, Dave and Ben, stared at the floor like naughty children who had just stolen a watermelon. While certainly these grown men weren't kids, they *had* stolen something. They had stolen their mother, literally.

Dorothy did not have Alzheimer's disease, but she had just enough memory loss to make her dangerous at home. She had left on burners at her house twice and an iron once. These men were sure their mother had done similar things much more often. She also was becoming increasingly frail from osteoporosis. She had fallen at least three times, twice suffering broken bones that required significant recovery periods. Still, Dorothy defiantly refused help—and that's what made the situation so difficult. She wouldn't let anyone other than her sons get into her house, and she refused to move where she could receive care. After she refused help and well-intentioned offers to help her make a move, she would get angry at her sons, accusing them of not caring for her properly.

Dave and Ben felt they had to do something—but what could they do? They cooked up a plan where Dave picked up Dorothy, telling her they were going to visit Ben. Instead of going to Ben's house, however, Dave took her to a personal care home he and Dave had rented on her behalf. This wasn't merely a bad solution; it was clearly illegal, since they had taken their mother against her will. They reasoned that their mother needed help and that she'd come to see that this new home wasn't so bad and make the adjustment. The personal care facility personnel rightly informed Dave and Ben that Dorothy was free to leave anytime she chose.

It wasn't that Dave and Ben were bad guys; on the contrary, their mother's health really was their primary concern. The problem was that, as a family, they had not communicated or achieved any movement on the issue of where Dorothy would live.

THE OPTIONS

What makes for a happy older person? You could just as well ask what makes for a happy person. Most of us like to have good relationships, good health, and the freedom to make our own decisions and live the way we deem best. The same is true for an older person.

As we said before, the reality is that relationships become fewer and fewer as friends move away or die, the older person's health starts deteriorating, and he or she becomes more limited in decision-making ability. Besides the emotional connection most of us have with home, it represents the last bastion of independence to which an older person can cling. As caregivers, we have to be thoughtful before we "storm the castle." It's good for us to first get a picture of all the available living options.

Hold It! Stay Right Where You Are!

Most homes or apartments are not designed with older people in mind. When an older person starts having difficulty with mobility, orientation, or health, home can feel more like an obstacle course than a safe haven. Still, for one reason or another, about five million older people will stay in their homes. Generally speaking, if you can safely keep your older parent in his or her own home, it's better for the family and better for the older parent emotionally. You'd do well not to get too excited about talking about moving when an older person first begins to have difficulty at home. With the proper modifications, an older person can stay in his or her home. These modifications can be of a physical or a service nature.

Physical Modifications

Physical modifications refer to changes made to a house or apartment to make it more user-friendly for older people. The number one threat to older people in their homes is injury due to falling, and the number one place where falls occur is the bathroom—not only because we use the bathroom so often but also because of so much bending, sitting down, and getting up on wet, hard surfaces.

Handrails around the toilet, tub, and shower can make a tremendous difference in increased safety. In addition, the toilet can be modified, either by replacing it with a taller model or using a raised seat on the existing toilet. A bathing chair in the tub or shower makes getting in and out much easier, as well as greatly reducing the chances of slipping on a wet surface. As a rule, taking a shower is much safer than taking a bath, so it's worth trying to reeducate your older parent who is used to bathing.

There are, however, special precautions one should take. Think about the many twists and turns a person makes under the showerhead—each poses a potential danger to an older person. This risk can be easily reduced by using a handheld showerhead. Nonskid mats or stickers inside the tub or shower also give the older person a secure surface when he or she is negotiating entries or exits. In addition, make sure all bath mats and area rugs are anchored securely and are as flat as possible.

The next most threatening area to older people is the kitchen. Many falls occur when older people bend down to get something out of a lower cabinet, but much more often they fall when they use a stool or chair to get something out of an upper cabinet. As a rule, a frail older parent shouldn't have anything in lower or upper cabinets; everything in the kitchen should remain easily within his or her reach. So what about family dishes or cooking utensils? Get rid of them, or store them. An older person usually cooks very simple food—if he or she cooks at all—and having all that "stuff" only tempts him or her to get at it at one time or another.

If your older parent is capable of cooking, you may consider changing the dials on the stove so they feature large lettering, or at least labeling the "OFF" position more clearly. It's worth purchasing appliances such as coffeemakers and warming ovens with automatic shutoffs. In addition, replace breakable dishes with unbreakable ones (injuries often happen during cleanup), and make sure all carpets, area rugs, and mats are secure.

In the rest of the home, make sure all carpets and area rugs are flat and secure as well. Take all belongings out of the upper shelves of closets and store them someplace out of sight. Remove unnecessary tables, lamps, or chairs that could serve as obstacles for someone with poor mobility or eyesight. In addition, consider replacing furniture with either higher sitting chairs or sofas, or even purchasing "lifting chairs" that can assist the older person in standing.

One physical modification often overlooked is the space itself. Consider closing off certain areas of the house that can be dangerous. Stairs that lead to lower and upper levels of the home almost always present a hazard to an older person, but simply telling him or her not to use the stairs seldom works. With the older person's permission—and if it's possible to do—consider locking the door leading to the lower level (make sure the key is unavailable to him or her), or build a permanent barrier that prevents access across the stairway to the upper level. If your older parent's house only has upper-level bedrooms, then convert a space on the ground level into a bedroom. While older people often resist this type of change, most see the wisdom in it if it allows them to stay in their own homes.

Finally, you could think about moving the older person to a smaller, more manageable home. My parents, in their mid-seventies and in good health, lived in a very old, large house with an upstairs and a basement. Although I tried to dissuade him many times, my father would not stop shoveling snow off the house's flat roof in the winter, and my mother could not resist crawling on ladders to patch cracks or put up new wall-paper. The house was simply too large and demanded too much upkeep—and it was a matter of time before one or both of my parents would have been injured.

My mother loved her house. It took a long time and many discussions—about three years' worth—but they finally concluded they'd live longer and healthier in a different house. They sold the massive, two-story, flat-roof house and bought an accessible, three-bedroom house with a sloped roof, which was much easier to maintain. Moving to a smaller, more manageable house or apartment often allows your older parent to maintain his or her independence.

Service Modifications

Service modifications can also allow an older parent who needs caregiving to stay in his or her home. Service modifications include requirements of daily living that used to be performed by the older parent but now are performed by family members, friends, or individuals or agencies for hire.

Overwhelmingly, most of the care provided for older people comes from their families. This arrangement can be especially taxing on the caregiver for several reasons. First, if you have a full-time job, you're probably finding it challenging enough to maintain one household; maintaining two households would be that much more difficult. Second, because older people who live in their own homes tend to have a singular focus (i.e., "my health, my food, my house"), they can be particularly demanding, making seemingly endless phone calls requesting your help and at times expressing great dissatisfaction. Finally, many times you simply don't have the skill or time required to give the care the older parent needs. Sometimes, hiring service providers to come into the home can be a way to keep your parent in his or her home without the situation becoming too overwhelming for you.

Service providers can range from housekeepers, to meals-on-wheels providers, to live-in companions. Two midrange options are a home personal care worker and a home health aide. Home personal care workers are usually provided through an agency and have received training on how to assist older people with both household and personal tasks. These workers can be hired for a certain number of hours a day and will do a variety of tasks—other than health care—during the allotted time. Many older people find if they have a little help—help getting up in the morning, dressing, bathing, preparing a meal—they can make it just fine.

Home health aides function more like nurse assistants. Although these workers, hired through agencies, can provide services similar to that of home personal care workers, they also provide some health services. Many of the agencies that offer the services of health aides also provide skilled nursing services. Registered nurses perform nursing tasks, often set up through a doctor's orders. When an older person requires such caregiving or nursing services for only a few hours a day, this approach can make sense. However, be aware that services provided for eight to ten hours a day will rival the costs of assisted living facilities.

It's possible to hire a nonagency worker to perform the tasks of a personal care worker or a health aide, but this person frequently lacks specific training in caregiving to older people. In the case of hiring a live-in companion, the worker pool is limited and an individual may not have the proper training or sensitivity. In all cases of hiring an outside person to stay in the home of your older parent, whether the person is from an agency or hired independently by you, it's best to take steps to protect your parent and his or her belongings.

Don't misunderstand me. Many who work in the caregiving field are wonderful people who give extraordinary care. But cases of abuse abound. You may want to drop in unannounced to find out the kind of care being provided. You should be watching for any signs of fear in your older parent regarding the caregiver, or any marks or bruises that could signal maltreatment. You should have valuables such as jewelry, silver, or precious objects removed from the house. Cash, credit card statements, and financial records should never be kept at your parent's house. This may seem overly cautious, but the stories are legion of people who have seen things "disappear" once their parent had an in-home caregiver (other than a family member). And once these objects or records disappear, they'll most likely never be seen again.

Recognize, too, that some people who pose as live-in companions find it easy to prey on the elderly. This person may try to convince your older parent that you are working against him or her. He or she may try to get your parent to put the companion's name on a checking account, assign him or her power of attorney, and talk your parent into changing his or her will, making the huckster the beneficiary. Watch out for the companion who draws abnormally close to your parent and who seeks to become "part of the family."

Let me reiterate, though, that many very honest and professional caregivers provide in-home services. The U.S. Administration on Aging, a governmental agency, has set up Area Agencies on Aging (AAA). You should be able to ask an AAA in your community or region to provide you with the names of reputable agencies or individuals who have a solid history of caregiving. Also, you can contact Eldercare Locator (1-800-677-116) and inform them of your need. This service will provide you with local and regional information on services and providers.

When Full-Time Care Is Needed

Before the last twenty-five years, if you had to leave your home as an older person, it usually meant living in a nursing home. As our society moved to dual-income households, however, another option developed. These are called assisted living facilities. The goal of these facilities is to keep the older person as free and as independent as possible, while offering various services such as meals, housekeeping, social activities, medication monitoring, and some access to medical care.

The low-end assisted living facility can best be described as a retirement facility or independent living units. Typically, these types of facilities either have small apartment cottages in clusters or small one- or two-room apartments under one roof. They usually have a central dining room that provides two or three meals a day, weekly housekeeping, and a variety of social programming. Although these facilities usually have staff present for a good part of the day (some twenty-four hours a day), they do not have personal care workers, health care aides, or nurses. Therefore, they offer no grooming or hygiene assistance, no medication monitoring, and no health care. It's fairly common for this type of facility to provide scheduled transportation. Usually call buttons or panic buttons are provided in case a resident needs help, but response is often limited to the staff on duty. The older person in this type of facility is expected to maintain independent apartment living with quite minimal supervision and service.

The most obvious advantage to this type of living arrangement is cost. It's a first step in services for an older parent without the enormous cost of full-time care. Your older parent can maintain his or her own apartment or cottage and still have privacy. Many of these facilities, while not providing care services, have good working relationships with home care or health care individuals or agencies. Therefore, you can have confidence that if care is needed, they'll know who to contact. But be aware that any extra care services will have to be paid for, just as these professionals would be paid if they came to your parent's home. And if your older parent's needs become more acute, or if your parent isn't a good fit with the facility, he or she can and will be asked to leave, most of the time within one month of notification (the typical lease period). Finally, these types of facilities are rarely regulated by the state or any agency. They function more as apartment facilities than as care providers.

The high-end assisted living facilities are often called personal care homes (or facilities). These facilities are regulated by the state and will be inspected every six to eighteen months. Most of them have one- or two-room apartments under one roof or clustered together in cottages, and they're furnished by the residents. In addition to the services provided at low-end assisted living facilities, these feature twenty-four hour staffing and usually have a nurse on duty for at least one shift during the day. These facilities are staffed by care aides who assist with bathing, dressing, and grooming, as well as housekeeping, laundry, and ambulation around the facility. Most of these personal care homes have someone on staff responsible for planning activities and coordinating scheduled transportation for residents.

Although personal care facilities can monitor and dispense medications, they cannot render medical assistance unless in an emergency. It's also important to realize that personal care facilities are designed to encourage the older person to be independent. The residents will be observed and supervised, but they are free to leave the facility. Most personal care homes have some type of security system that monitors when someone leaves the building, but staff-to-resident ratio is often not sufficient to know where every resident is at all times.

Costs of personal care facilities can vary dramatically, depending on the care required. When your parent moves in—and every few months or so thereafter—your older parent will typically be evaluated with regard to Activities of Daily Living. As he or she requires more personal care, the rent and care costs will invariably increase. It has become increasingly common for personal care homes to have a dementia or Alzheimer's unit. Many older people with dementia or Alzheimer's disease have no other medical condition requiring full-time nursing care, and so the personal care home is sometimes a good option. These units are staffed more fully and have trained personnel who know how to deal with people with this condition. Of course, the cost for these services increases significantly.

An additional option for care is a continuing care retirement community (or life care community). These communities often have single-family homes, independent living units, a personal care facility, and a nursing home, all at the same location. Residents move from one housing choice to another as their needs change. Many offer extravagant amenities, like a golf course and swimming pool, as well as several dining options and plans. What sets these facilities apart is that they often require a substantial entrance fee (anywhere from $20,000 to $250,000), as well as a monthly fee for the services the older person requires. With such a large financial commitment, you'll want to make sure the facility offers the services your older parent needs now *and* in the future. Check out the financial solvency of the facility, and ask if it is accredited by the Continuing Care Accreditation Commission (CCAC).

No matter what kind of assisted living facility you choose, there are several important factors to consider:

- Consider whether the services provided are what your older parent actually needs. The social activities and transportation may sound great, but these services are of no use if your parent doesn't take advantage of them.
- Be realistic in determining if the facility can provide care for your older parent for a significant period of time. If your older parent is deteriorating rapidly, it may not make sense to choose a type of care that's quite different from what your parent eventually may need.
- The facility should have a good reputation. Be sure to check with your Area Agency on Aging, the state's regulatory system, and present residents. If the facility is licensed, ask to see the last few inspection reports.
- Make sure the facility has a warm and nice feel to it. There should be a good combination of comfortable common areas and good privacy options for your parent.
- Check to see if the facility provides sound, consistent care. Go there and just hang out for a while, observing how the staff cares for the residents.
- Consider the entrance costs and monthly costs, and determine what are the conditions under which the agreement may be terminated.
- Make sure the facility is clean, organized, and service oriented.

Long-Term Care

Long-term care—typically nursing home care—is perhaps the most difficult care option to consider. We've all heard horror stories of nursing homes where residents went unmonitored and had needs unmet, where facilities looked dirty and smelled of urine. No doubt some of these facilities exist, but the majority are high-quality care facilities.

Long-term care is needed for an older person when his or her health has been compromised to the point of needing twenty-four-hour-a-day medical supervision, observation for mental disorders, or full-time observation for dementia or Alzheimer's disease.

Most long-term care facilities have either private or semi-private rooms and require residents to sleep in a hospital bed; many will allow a resident to bring a piece of furniture like a chair or dresser. In addition to having full-time nursing staff, the facility will have health care aides on staff as well. In general, most nursing homes have the same type of amenities as licensed personal care facilities, along with the ability to provide medical services and meals in rooms.

Since all nursing home facilities are regulated, you should be able to call your state's human resources division or health department to see if the home has had complaints or violations filed against it. Staffing patterns in nursing homes are very important, so watch for how staff members respond to resident needs—if they treat residents with respect—and if staff members seem satisfied in working at the facility. Although as a rule nursing facilities have a much sparser look to them because of ambulation issues associated with wheelchairs and hospital beds, it's reasonable to expect that the environment should be warm and clean.

Life with Mom and Dad

Caregiving in your home on an hourly and daily basis can be an emotionally rewarding and spiritually deepening experience. Great satisfaction comes in knowing that your older parent is well cared for in a warm environment surrounded by people who love him or her. But it can also be emotionally exhausting and just as expensive as other forms of care. If you are considering caring for a parent in your home, you should think carefully about several aspects of the relationship:

- Does my home need to be modified? It may need to be modified in ways similar to the modifications necessary to keep a parent in his or her own home. These modifications can be profound and expensive and may change your "safe haven" into a place not nearly as comfortable and relaxing.
- Is my home big enough to take on another member? If you plan to take away one of your children's rooms or convert a heavily used living space, your family is prone to see the caregiving task as a hardship.
- Do our family members possess the necessary skills to care for our parent? Many caregivers learn as they go, but not everyone can offer the skilled care required for every older person.
- What about the work and school schedules of family members? Will my older parent be left on his or her own for long periods of time?
- Is my family prepared emotionally for the task of caregiving? *I* may want to care for my parents in my home, but if my spouse or children don't support the idea, it may cause more emotional stress than is bearable.
- Will there be significant emotional wear and tear on you from the older parent? Many older people are a pleasure to be around, no matter their physical condition, but if you have unfinished business with your older parent, or if he or she is angry, threatening, or manipulative, caregiving may take more emotional energy than you possess.

I'm not suggesting an older parent should be cared for in the home only when it fits nicely into the caregiver's life. On the contrary, there are great connections and rewards that can come from this type of caregiving. I am suggesting, however, that you beware of wrong reasons to give care in the home.

If an older parent has made you promise—as many do—that you will never put him or her in a care facility, you need to realize the request was shaped by fear and an attempt to manipulate. The process of aging and having to be cared for is a scary and humbling thing. But it is also something intended to teach older people as much as it is to teach us. When an older person manipulates such a promise, he or she may well be saying, "I'm the most important person in this family. I am more important than you, your children, and your grandchildren." The parent is trying to stave off old age and the challenges it brings. You cannot protect your older parent from this fear, and you should never be asked to do so.

A sense of obligation, or duty, is a lousy reason to care for an older parent in your home—not the obligation that says, "I want to give him the care I feel he deserves," but the one that says, "She did it for her parent, so I guess it falls to me to care for her." Such obligation only builds frustration, which finally blossoms into resentment. This resentment fosters bitterness, which poisons the family legacy and makes impossible the experience of fulfilling relationships.

Caregiving is not a death march; it is a precious gift. Any of us involved with older parents are caregivers to one degree or another, and it's wrong to think that the only proper form of caregiving is the kind that takes place in your home.

It's possible to have a great caregiving experience in the home. Other relatives and friends can often offer support and respite. In many metropolitan areas, senior citizen centers and adult day care agencies offer additional services. But this type of caregiving should be undertaken only if there is a clear desire to do so and there's agreement on the part of the entire family.

Caregiving for an aging parent in your home is not just a matter of a desiring heart or a strong family commitment; it is also a matter of counting the costs and being sure you have enough resources to do the job.

What Care Is Appropriate or Best?

By assessing the Instrumental Activities of Daily Living and the Activities of Daily Living (see chapter 4), you should have some idea of the level of functioning your older parent currently possesses. What level of care is then appropriate or best?

At least to some degree, the level of care needed and the financial issues will determine housing choices. Information about financial issues will be covered in chapter 7. The following chart will give you an idea of housing options based on your older parent's need:

Older Person's Need	Care Alternatives
Needs help with Instrumental Activities of Daily Living (i.e., shopping, keeping finances, etc.)	Occasional help from family members
Needs help with bathing/showering	Occasional help from family members or health care aide or assisted living facility
Needs help with meal preparation, dressing, grooming	Daily help from family members or health care aide or assisted living facility
Needs help with medication regimen, including taking daily medications	Daily help from family members or health care aide or assisted living facility
Needs health monitoring or supervision due to cognitive impairment	Full-time care from family members or health care aide/live-in companion or assisted living facility or long-term care facility
Needs medical monitoring, interventions, or supervision due to emotional imbalance or wandering tendencies due to cognitive impairment	Full-time care from family members or health care aide/live-in companion or long-term care facility

MOVING OUT AND LEAVING HOME

Dorothy, the eighty-three-year-old woman with the adult sons, Dave and Ben, clearly met the criteria for needing some kind of daily help. While Dave and Ben had correctly assessed their mother's need, they had problems with execution. Not only did she need daily help now; chances were good she'd need *more* help in the fairly near future.

When you conclude an older parent needs some level of help, there are several things to consider:

Start Early

If as your parent gets older and there seems to be a good possibility he or she will need help in the future, it's almost certain he or she will. To sit back and hope you won't have to face the problem of securing help for your older parent is worse than taking up the dice in Las Vegas.

Your older parent will probably live far longer than you or he or she imagined. Future help isn't an issue that will go away, and so it's best to swallow hard and bring up the subject at an early enough point where you can include your older parent in the decision-making process.

It will be a relief to some older parents when you bring up the subject of care, for they already perceive the need. Most older parents recognize they are aging, and they have friends or spouses who have needed such care. These discussions can cover much ground quickly in determining a plan. Be aware, though, that some older parents have a built-in resistance to the idea of discussing care. Remember, denial can be a powerful thing.

Bring up the subject in a setting where your older parent cannot easily change the subject or leave the room. If your parent can hear well enough in the car, I've found it to be a good place to broach the subject. In some instances, I've recommended that people take their parents on a drive and pull over at a roadside park to have the discussion. If a car ride won't work, you may want to have the discussion in your home or in a restaurant. The idea is this: if you're on his or her turf, your older parent can easily deflect your discussion, take up other tasks, or go to another room.

Once you have your older parent in a place for a good discussion, it's best to be straightforward but not dictatorial. I suggest something like, "You're in good enough health now, Mom, but you've had enough trouble that I can see you may need help caring for yourself in the future. What thoughts have you had about getting some help if your health worsens?" This question isn't intended to ease into the subject; it is an anchor you must drop to get an answer. If your mom brushes aside the topic or tries to change the subject, you must make the anchor secure by refusing to discuss anything else before she has answered in some fashion.

Some will say, "I don't want to upset my parent." While these kinds of discussions can feel upsetting, they are a necessary part of life. If you start early enough—before care for your older parent is an immediate need—you can start breaking the ground a little at a time. Many times, your older parent will make a few statements about the kind of care he or she envisions, and then ask to discuss something else. This is a fair request, but make it clear that you will keep returning to the issue until a plan gets developed. As a general guide, plan on bringing up future care for an aging parent every four to six weeks until a secure plan is made.

Develop a Plan

When I met with Dorothy and her two sons, I told them I'd be happy to work with them, but I insisted that Dorothy be returned to her home so she could make her own choices. This was an important step to build trust with Dorothy, because she needed to believe that I was not part of a conspiracy to force her to move out of her home. But there was a twist. "Dave and Ben will take you back home," I said, "but you need to know that if you want them to help you in the future, you'll have to discuss the subject of your care and needs. It's not fair to expect you to move without careful discussion and planning, but it's also not fair to expect them to be responsible for your care but not get your cooperation."

Dorothy was slow to understand this because she wanted to tell the story over and over again how Dave and Ben had wronged her. Every time she told the story, I agreed with her but reiterated the need for her to discuss her care. She finally agreed to come back to see me the next week if she could return home that day. Although Dave and Ben were hesitant, they decided it was a necessary action in order to make progress.

In the next session, I asked Dorothy if she was back home. "They took me back home, but they haven't been back to see me [it had been three days], and I need some help."

"Tell me about the kind of help you need," I said.

Dorothy responded, "It'd be nice if I could have someone cook some meals and help me get around the house and get out to the store."

"So you've become aware that you have some needs you can't meet yourself?" I asked.

Dorothy quickly replied, "No, I can take care of myself."

"Then how often are you able to cook meals for yourself, and how do you get around to do your shopping?" I asked.

Dorothy avoided these questions and told me instead what she had eaten at her last meal. I immediately returned to the subject. "Dorothy, you said you can take care of yourself but you can use help with meals and getting around. How often do you cook, and how do you get around?"

We went back and forth four times before she blurted out, "I don't cook, and I do need some help, but I don't want anyone helping me!"

Many times, when older people sense they're losing control of their lives and their health, they become experts at avoiding the subject. Dorothy held much of the power in the relationship with her sons because she made a demand for care but also a demand for independence. She'd then refuse to talk about alternatives. I simply wouldn't let Dorothy avoid the subject. I camped on the question, and I taught Dave and Ben to do the same thing.

"No matter how many times your mother changes the subject," I instructed, "the essential question you must get answered is how you can get her the help she needs with no one helping her." I had Dave and Ben practice this over and over again, then sent them to a coffee shop to have the discussion. I agreed to see them the next day.

Dorothy and her sons came in the following day. "They did what you said. They wouldn't leave me alone. OK, I need some help, but they did it their way instead of mine."

We were now ready to discuss a plan. "Tell me your thoughts on the help you need and how you'll get it?" I asked.

Dorothy basically told me she wanted her sons or their wives to provide the help. Ben said, "We're happy to do things for you on the weekend, but we all work and you live forty miles from us. It's just not practical during the week."

So I asked Dorothy, "Do you have a solution to suggest?" Dorothy offered none, but I wouldn't let her leave the question unanswered. I asked three more times until she finally asked me for ideas. I replied, "These situations are always difficult. I know you want your independence, and your boys want you well taken care of. It's a hard thing to balance. But a possible balance is for you to stay at a personal care home during the week and then return home every other weekend with one of your sons so they could care for you."

Dorothy reacted with suspicion and asked many questions, but I kept saying, "It's just one idea to start you thinking about possible solutions." Although she didn't totally embrace the idea, it was a way to help her start thinking about moving from her home to get the necessary care.

As Dorothy began contemplating the idea of spending every other weekend at her home, Dave raised an important point. "It would be fine for Mom to keep her home for a while," he said, "but eventually, we're going to need the money to pay for her care at any place she moves to."

"Great!" I said. "Then go ahead and discuss that issue with your mother, remembering some of what you've learned before."

Dave stammered but finally got out, "We could keep your house for a while, but how would we pay for the care you eventually needed?" Dorothy again avoided the subject, but Ben took up the baton. "How would we pay for the care you will need?" Both Dave and Ben had learned their lessons well.

The key to making a plan is to stay focused on the difficulties and questions until they get adequately answered. Most people are capable of making a plan—they do it every day in their jobs and with their families. Yet with an older parent, frustration and the struggle over power dissuade them from making a plan. I simply taught Dave and Ben to avoid the power struggle and not do *anything* until Dorothy had discussed something.

In order to get the kind of help an older parent eventually needs, a plan must be developed by both the caregiver and older person. After three sessions, Dorothy and her sons did come up with a firm plan. Dorothy would move to the personal care home her sons had chosen, but she'd go to her home every other weekend with one of her sons until her home was sold. After that, she'd go to the home of one of her sons every other weekend. In this way, Dorothy got the care she needed *and* remained involved in the decision-making process.

Remember, Relationship Is the Most Important

Families tend to struggle over power—especially when it comes to issues of care and changing living situations. Often we get so focused on what we want to make happen and on what others are doing wrong that we tend to forget that relationships are precious and that all struggles are temporary.

On the fourth meeting with Dorothy and her sons, the plan had begun to be implemented. I encouraged the family to reconnect with their stories. "All of you are making progress toward solving the problems you brought in," I said, "but so often we just stop there and fail to connect with the most important things in life. Dorothy, you may think your sons are unfair at times; Dave and Ben, you may think your mother is sometimes unreasonable. You're both undoubtedly right. But the most important thing you can remember as you go through these changes is that it is not the house, the belongings, or the money that's important; it's your relationship with one another. What times speak well of your relationships with one another—times you want to remember despite this tough phase you've been going through?"

Dave and Ben spoke in generalities about their mother's dedication, but I kept pressing them to talk in specifics. Finally Ben said, "Mom was at every function we ever had as boys and most of the functions of our kids. She is loyal to us through and through." Dave and Ben related several stories of Dorothy's loyalty and faithfulness, and it clearly touched her. She remained fairly quiet through the session that was mixed with somber recollections and laughter, but she recalled something important toward the end.

"When your father died," she said, "he said he loved me like no other. I want you boys to know that, even though I'm difficult, I love you as no other."

The three left the session with arms around one another, laughing as they got into the car. Relationship and connection with the story—instead of the house and the power struggle—can make all the difference in the world.

Make no mistake, when we start letting go of our houses or apartments, our possessions, and eventually our independence, it is about our dying. It is about letting go and holding on to the only thing that will last—our relationship to a living and active God.

When Moses contemplated Israel's wandering in the desert, the frailty of his people as he watched an entire generation perish, he came to this conclusion, which is recorded in Psalm 90: "Lord, you have been our dwelling place throughout all generations" (verse 1). Moses went on to note that all we do perishes. His psalm has a decidedly depressing tone until he comes to the conclusion: "May your deeds be shown to your servants, your splendor to their children. May the favor of the Lord our God rest upon us; establish the work of our hands for us—yes, establish the work of our hands" (verses 16–17).

God is active and working among his people, Moses declares. Relationship is about story, and the story of our faith, our relationship with God, is the only thing that will have any weight with God. We want to hold on to many things, but the real value is not in what we lose throughout our lives—or in what we gain—but in the story of how we live. This is the story that interests God, and it's the story to which we should give our attention.

Deal with the Stuff

I not only worked at the personal care home; Sharon and I lived on the property. We saw it over and over again as people helped their older parents move in: tons of dressers, tables, beds, chairs—and no room in a one-room apartment. These older people had spent their lives accumulating stuff that was, for the most part, simply junk in the eyes of their children. It's the painful truth. None of your children will want your worn-out end tables or outdated recliners when you get ready to move. How painful it was as these older people realized their belongings would be shipped off to someone they didn't even know.

I've always been grateful that Genevieve never got trapped by her own "stuff." She lived very simply, and as far as I know, just about everything she owned that had some value or preciousness, she gave to her children. This testifies not only to the way she loved her children but also to the correct way she ordered her priorities. Stuff never had a hold on her and never consumed any more of her investment than was necessary.

Prepare to Close Down the Home Place

Whether the choice is to move into a family member's home, an assisted living facility, or a nursing home, there's a pretty good likelihood your older parent will experience a move from his or her home. Even though places consist of wood, bricks, and plaster, they pulsate with memories—some of which are good and some of which are bad. But like the stories that bind us together, homes are stories in and of themselves.

My mother, a child of the Great Depression, remembers her first house as a child: a two-room shack on the harsh plains of New Mexico. When as a boy we moved into the house she and my dad would occupy for some thirty-five years, I knew the house fulfilled many of her dreams. She loved the way it looked, felt, and aged. She loved fixing it up and remodeling it. She loved it because it represented everything she didn't have growing up—and it was more than she ever imagined she would live in.

But my mother was also a woman of courage. As she grew older, she knew she couldn't stay in the house forever, and my contentions that it was unsafe for her and my father eventually made sense. She gave a large part of its contents away and arranged for most of the family to be there for the final move. When it was time to leave, it was only right to honor the memory. On the last night in the house, we gathered around the table for a final meal. All sixteen of us, huddled in close, ate the favorite recipes and recalled the old stories. We still recall the old stories today, but on that night they came alive in the home where we had spent so many years. We ate, talked, laughed, and cried long into the night. And then we prayed.

Whatever the ritual we choose—last toasts, final dinners, prayers of remembrance—the homes of our older parents deserve a dignified parting. It helps us when we move our older parent from his or her place, but it also helps us gather in the memories so they'll stick in our minds like cobwebs.

HELP, HOME, AND PRECIOUS MEMORIES

It was a most difficult day. One very bad day in a progression of two weeks of bad days.

Genevieve had been doing fairly well in a personal care home for two years, but during the summer she started deteriorating more rapidly. Somehow the summers had never seemed quite so bad. But during a particular two-week period, she had concluded somehow that someone was going to pick her up every afternoon. By this time in her disease, she had lost us, her sense of time, and her sense of place. She just wanted to go—anywhere.

In many ways, it's true for all of us. We all want someone to pick us up in our confusion when we're lost, when we can't make sense of our place, when we no longer know anyone's name, when the world becomes totally unrecognizable. We desire somebody, anybody, to take us away. To put us in the passenger seat of a warm car and take us to a place where we belong. That was all Genevieve wanted.

As soon as the afternoon started, she would make her way to the front door and either bang on it or set off the door alarm. If successful in escaping the home, she'd wander aimlessly in the parking lot, trying to find an unlocked door to get into a car. The staff of the personal care home concluded she needed someone with her full-time in the afternoon—a task for which they were not equipped. So they would call us. This went on for two weeks.

We tried a medication adjustment, but we all knew it probably wouldn't work. Her current obsession could last two more weeks or two more years. As I made the drive to the personal care home, consumed by the tasks of finding an Alzheimer's unit, a new place to live, financial concerns, the details of another move, I felt an almost singular focus come on me. All I needed to do was to get to the home and care for Genevieve. Just be with her.

In her lost eyes, in her confusion, she still knew we were connected, even if she did not know how. It was a privilege. It was precious. It was a moment in time that we shared in simple warmth and tenderness. At that moment we shared a common struggle and a common goal: to simply be with and belong to one another. It remains one of the more precious times in my life.

I don't mean to minimize the problems with finding the right care or the concerns about where our older parents will live; but the reality is, these problems will not last. During these times of confusing problems and concerns, we have to learn to recognize these precious moments so we can write them permanently on our hearts. It is the basis of our memories—not so much the thoughts but the emotions we feel that make up the memory. This is what we hold.

The laughter of Christmases gone by. The joy of feeling overwhelmed at the birth of a child. The devastation of losing a loved one. Preciousness comes only through emotional connection. If you are wandering through life, wishing your life could count for something, you must make emotional connections. If you wander through the process of caregiving without capturing these precious memories, then indeed you are not making a connection; you are merely doing a job.

There have to be moments of preciousness in caregiving. By and large, you cannot make these moments. You must wait for them to happen. And to your delight, you may find that helping your older parent move to the next level of care, beginning the final journey of caregiving, can provide an opening for one of these precious moments.

QUESTIONS FOR CONSIDERATION

1. What living situations will best fit your older parent's need for caregiving?

2. If your parent resists discussing caregiving needs, in what context could the communication best take place?

3. How can you make an emotional and relational connection with your older parent as you both go through the process of securing the necessary care?

6

Where Is the Kitchen?
Dementia and Alzheimer's

And just as we have borne the likeness of the earthly man,
so shall we bear the likeness of the man from heaven.
1 Corinthians 15:49

As Genevieve started slipping away, we often took her to the doctor just to help evaluate the progression of her disease. On one such trip, Sharon learned there would be a significant wait, so she took her mother on a short walk around a residential neighborhood. While walking, she saw an older middle-aged woman pull into a driveway. The garage door opened, and another woman, obviously the mother, came out and greeted her daughter. As the mother got into the car, they both laughed and headed out—perhaps toward a fun-filled time of dinner and shopping, or maybe to a grandchild's birthday party.

For Sharon, it could not be; it would never be again. She had enjoyed such times with her mother before, but Alzheimer's disease had robbed her of any further opportunities. It had put a cruel end to the joy. Now there was just the pain of trying to finish life.

It's a funny thing about losing someone to dementia or Alzheimer's in this day of modern geriatric medicine. We lose them slowly. It's not that our sweet memories of them vanish, because the memories are still there, locked away in our psyche. But we also feel keenly the present pain of the situation. We are left to do the work of getting our older person to the finish line of life the best we know how, yet we're still stricken with the grief of all that has been lost.

No one can quite describe the pain of having your parent, who has loved you with all of his or her heart, look at you and not have the slightest idea who you are. It is a slow, excruciating grief, something like pulling off an enormous Band-Aid wrapped around your heart—but you don't get it yanked off quickly with one sharp pain; rather, it gets pulled off slowly and painfully over many years. Sometimes it hurts so regularly you begin to think of the process as normal.

Eventually you become numb to it. And then, in the most innocent of times—taking a walk with your mother and seeing another mother and daughter having fun, for example—you realize how long and how awful the pull of the Band-Aid over your heart has been. It does more than make you cry; it injures every part of you that has grieved silently for years. But it also makes you cry because you know the Band-Aid still hasn't come off. It will continue to be pulled and ripped in that slow but constant motion, and with it, part of your heart comes off too. And you have no idea how long it will last. Perhaps another day. Perhaps another week. Perhaps another decade. It is grief by inches when hundreds of miles lie ahead.

Dementia and Alzheimer's disease present some of the most devastating problems a caregiver can ever face. Dementia is a broader term that, in essence, means a person loses his or her cognitive processing ability, judgment, perception, and ability to focus on daily tasks of living. Most cases of dementia are caused by Alzheimer's, a disease that renders neuronal cells useless and eventually kills the person by slowly exterminating the thinking and functioning processes of the brain.

The other primary cause of dementia is death of neurons due to a stroke that cuts off blood supply to certain areas of the brain. The loss of memory and functioning in these cases usually is not progressive, although many older people experience a series of small strokes over a long period of time.

The odds of getting Alzheimer's disease aren't so high at the beginning of the aging process. Only three or four percent of people in their sixties and seventies develop the disease. Recent research has even shown that we can ward off Alzheimer's by keeping our brains active and engaged in our thirties, forties, and fifties. Newer medications seem to stem the tide of the disease, slowing down memory loss. All of this is very encouraging when we consider how debilitating the disease is to the family. But all the news is not good.

As we age, chances of developing Alzheimer's increase dramatically. About one out of every two persons aged eighty-five and older develop some form of dementia. Alzheimer's causes most of this dementia. Of course, this is the group of aging people that will most likely need care. Chances are quite good that you will have to face some form of dementia over the course of your parent's deterioration.

How Do You Know If It's Alzheimer's?

No one knows what causes Alzheimer's, and no test has yet been developed that can confirm your older parent has the disease. Only an autopsy can positively reveal its presence. Researchers have, however, made great progress by using a complex technique of brain scans and chemical injections to actually see the plaques, twists, and tangles of the neurons. This has helped to determine which medications can effectively treat Alzheimer's, but it's too expensive to be used in identifying the disease. Current diagnosis involves a process of noticing common symptoms, doing mental exams, and ruling out other possible causes of impaired thinking and memory. The major warning signs of Alzheimer's include the following:

- *Memory loss affecting job skills.* They forget job tasks or get confused on the job.
- *Difficulty performing familiar tasks.* They forget what they're doing, such as preparing a meal. They become confused and distracted with tasks they formerly accomplished with little problem.
- *Problems with language.* Their language sometimes doesn't make sense. They forget words or have words "on the tip of their tongues."
- *Disorientation with time and place.* They become lost easily, even around such common and familiar locations as work or home. They may get confused as to current location.
- *Poor or decreased judgment.* They make poor or unsuitable choices, such as wearing inappropriate clothes (e.g., using a bathrobe as a coat).
- *Problems with abstract thinking.* They forget or have trouble with simple calculations that formerly posed no problem.
- *Problems misplacing things.* They lose things often but also place objects in inappropriate places (e.g., placing a purse in the refrigerator). They have no idea how objects get in these places.
- *Mood and behavior changes.* They have frequent mood swings for no apparent reason or develop new and inappropriate behaviors.
- *Personality changes.* They experience dramatic changes in personality, such as becoming anxious and paranoid, when formerly they acted in a calm and easygoing manner.

- *Loss of initiative*. They have diminished interest in activities and withdraw or are uninvolved in things that formerly brought great enjoyment.

If your older parent demonstrates some of these warning signs, you should seek help from a doctor. Keep in mind that some forms of dementia can be reversed. Be aware, too, that some drugs or misuse of medications can cause dementia. A doctor can also run a series of blood and urine tests to see if any detected deficiencies or abnormalities may be causing loss of function. If no cause is found, an MRI scan of the brain can determine if damage due to stroke has occurred. Some neurologists will order a spinal tap to see if an infection may be causing the disturbance. In about one in ten cases, causes other than Alzheimer's are responsible for the mental deterioration, in which case the problems can often be reversed.

Once any alternative causes are ruled out, a professional may order a mental status exam, which measures how the older parent handles tasks such as doing math calculations, counting backwards, remembering words after some time has passed, stating information about current events or dates, and drawing familiar objects like the face of a clock. In the case of impaired performance, another exam will probably be scheduled after several months have passed. If thinking and functioning continue to deteriorate, the likely diagnosis is Alzheimer's disease.

Some promising new drugs are treating the symptoms of Alzheimer's and slowing its progression. But let's be clear: there currently is no cure for Alzheimer's. The disease can progress quickly or slowly but usually has a three- to ten-year course of progression. (Early onset of Alzheimer's—in a person's forties or fifties—is rare and usually progresses more quickly.) You should also be aware that some genetic links to Alzheimer's disease have been discovered. If your parent develops Alzheimer's, you may be more likely to have the disease one day.

Alzheimer's progresses in stages, but the stages aren't always clear. It can be something like the way I get into a swimming pool—slowly, with my feet brushing the water. Then I step in and progressively creep out until the water gets higher and higher, up to my chest. At some point I'm definitely more in the water than out, but I got to that point only gradually. With Alzheimer's, there are points where you can definitely recognize a particular stage, but the progression to that stage will likely have been gradual.

Professionals have different descriptions of the stages of Alzheimer's. I typically think of it in three basic phases:

- *First phase*. In this stage, those afflicted with Alzheimer's likely have progressive memory loss and have a hard time finding the right words in conversation. They also may experience some substantial changes in their mood, and they may lose interest in normal activities or hobbies.
- *Middle phase*. As they progress in the disease, they will likely have difficulty making decisions about clothing or eating. Their mood swings will increase, as will problem behaviors such as anger, agitation, anxiety, or wandering. Speech and language problems will likely increase, as well as difficulty with coordination in walking, dressing, or eating. Short-term memory will normally have ceased to function, and they'll forget the names of friends and formerly familiar places such as their church.
- *End phase*. In this phase, their cognitive processes have deteriorated to the point where function is undependable. Mood swings and language will not make sense, nor will they be connected to anything

in particular. Coordination deteriorates, and they'll eventually lose the ability to perform motions such as walking or eating. Long-term memory eventually is erased, and they will no longer recognize you or any other person. In this stage they are vulnerable to other diseases or infections that may cause death, but they'll eventually die as the Alzheimer's progressively eliminates the brain's ability to control such basic body functions as respiration and heartbeat.

There is simply no other way to put it: Alzheimer's is a mean disease. It's hard to watch the slow, progressive deterioration and harder still to give care to an older parent who no longer connects with you in any significant way. Yet, even though it's difficult, caregiving for a parent with Alzheimer's has the power to teach us and to change our lives.

CAREGIVING AND ALZHEIMER'S

Mary was eighty-six and her daughter Joan was in her early fifties. Although Mary had functioned independently for many years, she had progressive difficulty eating regularly, taking care of her hygiene needs, and staying connected to friends. Joan and her sister made two trips to see Mary and had her evaluated by several doctors. Over the course of about five months, Mary was diagnosed with Alzheimer's and the decision was made to move her to Joan's house, where she would receive care.

"It's hard for me to believe this is Mom," Joan said. "I've never seen her speak a harsh word to anyone, and now she's threatening to hit me and yells at me every time I try to help her. We've never really been close, but my mother has always been appreciative. Now all I get from her is either total silence or anger."

Joan had nearly come to the end of her rope and felt at a loss to know how to communicate with and care for her mother. When I asked Mary about Joan's description of her behavior, she remained silent for a while, withdrew, and finally quipped, "I don't remember."

Physical Care

As Alzheimer's progresses, certain physical needs become evident. Memory loss is typically one of the first recognizable symptoms. Joan would say, "Mom doesn't realize it, but she will go in the kitchen to cook something and leave things out of the recipe or leave the burners on. When I ask her about it, she'll say something strange like, 'Where is the kitchen?'"

This is called *short-term memory loss*, and it refers to our functional memory, which keeps us on task to remember a phone number before we dial, where we are headed when we go to the closet to get our coat, or what has been said in recent conversations. All of us deal with short-term memory problems when too many things are on our minds or we get interrupted regularly. In Alzheimer's, the short-term memory ability itself gets destroyed.

At a minimum, this short-term memory loss can be an inconvenience. But it can also be dangerous. You can deal with it in the initial stages with simple reminders and by helping your older parent do certain tasks. Some have tried to make lists for their older parents, but this will work only in the very initial stages, because the person will likely forget to refer to the list. Deterioration in short-term memory will eventually call for supervision.

Doing daily tasks and knowing where you are both require short-term memory. Short-term memory loss is a major contributor to wandering and getting lost. Since Mary lived with Joan, Joan would have to plan on checking on and supervising her mother as Mary worsened.

Loss of coordination becomes another progressive problem with most older people suffering from Alzheimer's. In the initial to middle phases, the loss results in an inability or difficulty in performing everyday complex tasks. For instance, your parent may have difficulty putting toothpaste on a brush, putting the cap back on, and then brushing her teeth. He or she may have joints that stiffen and as a result become less flexible, so that bending, getting up, or even walking may become more difficult. As your parent progresses into the late-middle and end phases of the disease, he or she may forget how to do (or be unable to perform) even simple tasks, like buttoning a button or picking up an object. It's important for your older parent to maintain as much movement and flexibility as possible, which necessitates repetition of tasks, daily movement, and daily exercise.

My mother-in-law, Genevieve, was an ambitious walker throughout her life. Most days, she would walk three to five miles. Although doing so kept her flexible and in fairly good shape, we also found we had to give her tasks that would keep her hands and arms active. Sharon would often have Genevieve help with cooking or cleaning tasks, even though it would have been much easier to do the task alone. Intentional exercise, such as low-impact stretching of muscles and loosening of joints, is also helpful.

Incontinence is a problem for many older people, and it almost certainly will become one for people with Alzheimer's. This poses a particular challenge because supervision of toileting becomes necessary. It's good to progressively help your parent with such tasks as dressing and bathing so that he or she can get adjusted to you being present during formerly private tasks. Because wearing protective briefs will probably become necessary, you or another caregiver will have to check the briefs regularly and help your parent change when necessary. If your parent has become accustomed to your assistance, he or she will likely allow you to help in this most personal of tasks. Incontinence can be caused by a variety of factors, so it's good to have a thorough examination to make sure your parent can stay continent as long as possible.

Mood Swings and Behavior Changes

Of all the problems of care, perhaps the most difficult to cope with are the mood swings. Remember that Alzheimer's attacks the brain. In many ways, it's like a brain injury; affected people are apt to radically change behaviors and personalities. This radical change is not due, as some have thought, to latent desires and impulses masked in younger years. The dramatic damage inflicted on the brain by Alzheimer's can substantially alter the person's former personality and behavior.

These mood swings can vary tremendously from person to person. Some older people become extremely apathetic, while others become agitated. Extreme apathy may result in your older parent taking no interest in his or her former activities and profoundly reducing his or her communication. He or she may stop eating and desire to sit or sleep for long periods of time. Extreme agitation may manifest itself in constant, rapid, or repetitive movement or motion. Many older people keep on the move because of excessive energy. Agitation frequently includes angry and aggressive outbursts. Sometimes the older person will have a catastrophic reaction in which he or she verbally or physically attacks another person for no apparent reason. Don't forget that many older people with Alzheimer's may be quite robust and strong physically. You may not think an eighty-five-year-old can pack a punch, but many caregivers have been seriously injured by their older parent.

Some older people may become very anxious and even paranoid. Activities like constantly checking watches or clocks, hiding objects to protect them from others, and refusing to cooperate with someone may occur. In the case of any mood swing and personality change, the emotions are very real to the older person. It may be true there's no reason to feel frightened, but this fact doesn't lessen the older person's fear. These unruly emotions call for your support and understanding. Frustration with your older parent will likely cause more disturbing emotions and won't necessarily create a change in behavior.

Although these personality changes and mood swings require your support, most treatment options call for medication. Psychotropic drugs are often prescribed to change brain functioning and moods. Generally, the older brain does not function like a middle-aged brain. Since many of these medications were originally tested on a younger population, it's possible some drugs may only complicate personality changes and moods; some may even cause damage. But most psychotropics have been available for years and have been used successfully by psychiatrists on older people. As a result, most reactions are much more predictable.

Some mood swings and personality changes can be managed by altering the environment. Gentle encouragement can sometimes get an apathetic older person involved, while calming music and isolation can help with agitation. As the disease progresses, however, your older parent may require a mood-altering drug to help manage behavior—which can benefit both the caregiver and the older person. At one point in the progression of Genevieve's disease, she slept only about two hours a night, which complicated her already high anxiety. Medication helped calm her and allowed her to get a good portion of the rest she needed.

Unless another disease or an infection kills your older parent, he or she will eventually become totally dependent as a result of Alzheimer's. Over 80 percent of older parents with Alzheimer's receive care at home. Many of these families, however, eventually opt for assisted living or long-term care as the disease progresses to the end phase.

While there are advantages to keeping an older parent with Alzheimer's at home, many Alzheimer's units and nursing facilities are uniquely suited to the demands of such intense caregiving. As a caregiver, you should carefully evaluate the demands of care in relationship to the other demands in your life, as well as your physical and emotional ability to provide ongoing care. You don't need to feel guilty if you opt for a care facility for your older parent. Comparisons with other people and situations are unwise and unproductive, as each situation is different. Don't let others (or yourself) pile on guilt for making this type of decision.

Issues of Power and Control

Research clearly shows that happiness and well-being among older people is tied to independence—which makes sense, because most of us feel happiest when we have our independence. Alzheimer's, however, robs the older person of this independence. With the loss of independence comes the loss of the power to choose—and this also applies to the caregiver.

Consider two of the primary difficulties in caring for an older parent with Alzheimer's: (1) the gradualness of deterioration and (2) the gradient of caregiving. An older parent with this disease tends to lose control and abilities very slowly. As a result, he or she initially retains a large part of the thinking and processing abilities he or she always did. Therefore, it can be difficult for the older parent to adjust to the intrusion of a caregiver. On the other hand, the caregiver usually sees much more of the deterioration (and needed care) than does the older person. In the beginning stages of the disease the older person will want and will be able to maintain significant control and independence. As the disease progresses, however, the caregiver need will increase. As that gradient increases, the older person will become more dependent on the caregiver and will lose more control. At some point the caregiver is in control and the older person is completely dependent, but it can be challenging to find a working balance in the initial and middle phases of Alzheimer's.

I was sure an issue of power and control caused the primary difficulty between Joan and Mary. Mary was accustomed to making her own choices and being independent. She felt fairly enthusiastic about moving in with Joan, but she regarded Joan's efforts to help as intrusions. Joan would offer to brush Mary's hair when it obviously needed straightening, but Mary would grab the brush and snap, "Don't!" while pointing the brush in Joan's face.

In such situations, it's important to get help on several fronts. Ask yourself whether a mood swing may be contributing to the power struggle. If an older person feels agitated, caregiving will likely only cause conflict. The environment may need to be changed, but medication may also be required. In this situation, it wasn't so much a mood swing as the fact that Mary wanted independence.

"You're a very independent woman," I said to Mary. "Joan told me you were a librarian before you retired and were responsible for government documents. That's a big job!"

"It *is* a big job," Mary answered. "I manage all the daily things that need to be put out and all the laws and things." Mary knew she had worked at the library but couldn't find the words for the things she had done. For instance, she couldn't come up with the word *periodical*. What's more, she stated things in the present tense, which indicated that Mary was in the late-initial stage of Alzheimer's.

"I would imagine you have to know how to do many things to be a librarian," I said.

"Oh yes," she responded, "you have to know how to keep things straight—be organized."

When older people need more care, they often do better accepting help when they can give some as well. I thought if Mary could contribute something to the household to help Joan, she'd be more likely to accept Joan's care. I asked Mary, "What are some things you think Joan could do to get her house organized?" Mary clearly had the library in mind. "She could get her books in order." I accepted this and made a plan with Joan and Mary to clean up Joan's bookcases. Joan would take the books off the shelf and ask Mary to help her arrange the books in the proper "organized" fashion.

The next session, Joan told me how it had gone.

"She ordered me around a lot," she reported. "I had to keep us on task, but we got two shelves completely done."

"Does it look better?" I asked.

"Sure," Joan said. "If there's one thing Mom knows, it's books."

I looked at Mary, who was obviously pleased, and said, "So you did some good work!"

"Like she said," Mary replied, "I know books."

When power and control begin to shift from older person to caregiver, it helps to frame the work, as much as possible, in terms of "companioning" or "doing things together." For example, instead of telling the older person that his or her hair needs combing and then proceeding to do the job, I prefer a statement like, "Would you help comb the back of *my* hair?" After the older person makes the effort to help, there exists a companioning opportunity to say, "Thanks! Now let me pay you back by getting the back of your hair."

I encouraged Joan to employ this very technique. "What's the most difficult task you and your mother have?" I asked her.

"Probably getting her to take her medication," Joan replied.

I asked Joan if she also took some daily medication—and she told me she took two pills each day.

"Then I'd like you to set out the medications for both your-self and Mary each morning, and loosen the tops of the bot-tles," I told her.

I turned to Mary and asked, "Would you be willing to help Joan get her medication out when you get yours?" She said yes, so I looked at Joan and said, "Then you instruct her on how many pills to take out, just like she instructed you where to put the books on the shelf. After the meds are out, try tak-ing them together."

Joan came back the next session and said, "I can't believe what a difference this made. We had only one tussle over the meds this week, and I think it was because I was pushing too hard."

In this transition of power and control, it's wise for the care-giver to remember that the older person is not a child who must passively accept care. Even though caregivers of a child and of an older person share some common tasks, the two roles are very different. When you change the diaper of a baby, the baby is an infant. When you change the briefs of an older parent, he or she is an emotional adult, whether or not he or she has impaired ability. Long past the time the cogni-tive functioning of an older person may decline, he or she retains this emotional functioning. When you insult older per-sons by treating them like infants, they will often respond in an angry or agitated fashion.

I don't believe a role reversal occurs in the care of older parents. A parent teaches an infant or child almost everything the little one is learning about life. The parent is responsible for a huge part of a child's personality development. Care-givers never carry out this same task for their parents, even though they may feed them or bathe them. The older person remains an adult, and we do a better job as caregivers if we respect and honor that adulthood, no matter the specific kind of care we give.

With this in mind, I urged Joan to consider Mary, not as a child in need of care, but as an adult who needed assistance. The attitude shift made a world of difference to Mary and made good caregiving possible.

Emotional Caregiving

Unlike the victim of a massive stroke, who loses physical abilities or memories, the person who develops Alzheimer's knows very well what is happening to him or her. Put yourself in the place of an older parent who notices day by day his or her faulty memory. Imagine what it would feel like to hear you have a disease that will eventually strip away your very identity long before you die. Try to understand how it feels to know you will eventually become dependent on your family or on someone you love. Receiving a diagnosis of Alzheimer's is a difficult thing. Though it's a huge challenge for a caregiver, think of the ramifications for the older person.

It helps me to think in terms of the emotional challenges an older person with Alzheimer's faces. In the initial phase, the older person notices his or her lost capacity, faulty memory, or inability to perform familiar functions. He or she will likely receive a diagnosis and start the process of planning for caregiving. Most older people I deal with in these situations have a tremendous fear of the future, deny what is really happening, and get depressed over their eventual demise. Estimates of the number of people who become depressed over a diagnosis of Alzheimer's range as high as 50 percent.

In the middle phase of the disease, the older person needs more and more care as he or she can no longer perform many tasks. The faces of family members, friends, and other acquaintances may become unrecognizable, and the person becomes aware something is wrong—without being able to decipher exactly what it is.

In the final phase of Alzheimer's, the victim progressively loses his or her sense of self as memories and self-awareness fade into darkness. Eventually the older person becomes incapacitated and totally dependent.

How do we care for an older parent who is experiencing this kind of emotional upheaval? The closest I can come to putting myself in the place of someone with this terrible disease is to imagine myself as a soldier caught in a battle I didn't choose and one from which I cannot escape. In this battle, every move I make, whether it's defensive or aggressive, results in a decreased capacity to fight—with no victory possible and death my only certainty. How would I respond? Most likely with denial, fear, or depression. The only thing that could make the awful process bearable is the loving presence of another human being.

What can we do for our older parent as he or she negotiates this awful disease? We can offer the comfort of our presence. And we can do so in at least three practical ways:

- *Helping our older parent face the truth.* "Each of you must put off falsehood and speak truthfully to his neighbor," the apostle Paul tells us, "for we are all members of one body" (Ephesians 4:25). We're often tempted to deny death or sickness, but when others around us acknowledge the truth and get mobilized to love and support us, we find the denial tougher to make. On occasion, some people won't allow others to support them because they operate under the assumption that the sickness or the loss they experienced belongs only to them. I recently worked with a young man suffering from a brain tumor who wouldn't allow anyone around him to acknowledge his sickness. "I don't want that negative energy around me," he said. To the contrary, being truthful about sickness and death helps to create positive energy as we do the only thing we can do in a tough situation: hold on to one another and love one another because we function as members of one body. In other words, we are all in this together. This doesn't necessarily mean we solve all of our older parent's problems; it simply means that, by our presence, we take on the truth of his or her situation and refuse to abandon him or her, thereby showing we are one in Christ.

• *Doing whatever is necessary.* "If anyone has material possessions and sees his brother in need but has no pity on him, how can the love of God be in him? Dear children, let us not love with words or tongue but with actions and in truth" (1 John 3:17–18). The tragedy of Alzheimer's is that it takes away our ability to do the most basic things, such as eating, dressing, and toileting. When Jesus saw a need, he didn't ring bells or call attention to his simple acts of service. His service did, however, made an indelible mark on his followers. Our presence gives emotional support when we button a dress, clean up a mess from diarrhea, or give a spoonful of food. Practical, nitty-gritty action in the face of unpleasant physical needs assures an older person that he or she will never be alone.

• *Being in the moment.* "Rejoice with those who rejoice; mourn with those who mourn," says Paul in Romans 12:15. The course of Alzheimer's disease often calls for tears; but even in the midst of tragedy, we also find numerous times to rejoice.

After Mary and Joan started working together more effectively, I taught Joan to connect with what remained of Mary's memory. Alzheimer's usually attacks the short-term memory in the early stages, but the long-term memory stays intact much longer. The long-term memory records significant past experiences and emotions, such as catching a winning touchdown pass or having a baby.

In caregiving we tend to focus only on what needs to be done at the moment. But just as important, both to us and to the older person, is to make connections with the past in which we shared important emotions. I asked Joan to bring in several family photographs. As we looked through the pictures, I paid particular attention to those in which Mary made a connection. One picture showed Joan's sister and Mary, just after Joan's sister was born. As Mary looked at the picture of herself holding the new baby, I began to ask questions.

"Mary, where was your daughter born?"

"She was born where we live—in Baton Rouge," she replied. "She was full of colic and kept me and Hank [her husband] up a lot."

I proceeded to ask Joan about her own children. She described some of the challenges she had faced as a new mother and reported that Mary had helped her in the weeks after her children were born.

"One time I remember when my oldest son was a few days old," Joan said. "Mom and I were standing at the crib. My mom slipped her arm around me and told me how special I was. I've never forgotten that moment."

Mary gazed at Joan for a long moment, who teared up and wiped her eyes. Mary looked lovingly at Joan and said, "You are still my special one." With misty eyes, Joan embraced her mother.

How far can you get as you journey through the tough times of Alzheimer's? The answer—at least, for a good portion of the disease—is as far as every pleasant memory can take you. Connecting with the long-term memories and sharing the emotional joy are good for the older parent and the caregiver alike. The moments of laughter, as well as the moments of tears, join our hearts together.

How about You?

Caregiving for an older parent is a long and arduous task in which you can count on experiencing emotional upheaval. Understand that you will have feelings and emotions that must be dealt with. You must cope with a variety of things, but let me suggest three that consistently come up as I work with families.

Communication

As Genevieve's disease entered the final stage, words became less and less frequent. I would sit on a bench next to her, sometimes for hours, without her saying a word. She would try to say something every now and then, but words simply had vanished. She had lost the ability to make connection through communication.

Have you ever pondered how much we depend on verbal communication? We see nonverbal signs, and sometimes we can read the emotional communication hidden in facial expressions and body postures. But we still depend on verbal communication to confirm what people know and feel. Everything else is simply a guess.

Alzheimer's robs the person of this verbal communication. Language disappears—a bit at a time. And the more time that goes by, the more we wonder what goes on inside the person's head. I have heard many times, "I wonder what is going on behind those blank eyes." Soon we find that verbal communication simply grinds us to a halt. We cannot discuss the future, because there's none to look forward to. We cannot communicate about the past, because the memory is gone. We become stuck between words—not because we've been struck speechless but because we can go no further, almost as though the person is no longer there.

It is in their presence—between the words—that we have to search for the part of his or her humanness that still bears the image of God. As the apostle Paul wrote, "And just as we have borne the likeness of the earthly man, so shall we bear the likeness of the man from heaven" (1 Corinthians 15:49). Before our eyes, even when we find it hard to believe, this older parent with blank expression and little or no verbalization skills is in the process of being transformed into the likeness of Christ. The fact is, our older parent is much closer to becoming Christlike than we are, since he or she is much closer to physical death.

To help us bear our frustration at the lack of communication, we must remember the words of the past—wisdom spoken by our older parent during our time of need, love given when we were alone. But even more, we need to look forward to the wisdom and love he or she will share with us in the kingdom of heaven, where no deteriorating minds or bodies will limit our communication. Our parent, who is to be wholly a part of the church triumphant, has a little of that part even now. It is that part we hold on to—to have and to hold, however long we have them. For though we will lose them physically, we will never completely lose them emotionally. In the absence of communication, we must comfort ourselves with this truth.

Grief

I encounter many couples in marriage counseling and individuals who are recovering from grief over the death of a spouse. Without a doubt, the grief one feels over divorce is much more complicated than grief due to death. Divorce has more unanswered questions, and the pain remains an open wound because the divorced spouse still lives and can potentially cause further problems. In much the same way, grief over a parent with Alzheimer's is more complicated than grief over death. In the final stages of Alzheimer's, the person who was your older parent is no longer there. The quirks of personality, the sense of humor, the loving spirit of your parent all have somehow slipped away. Yet your parent's body is still with you. We do not hold funerals for living people, and yet we experience profound and complicated grief over them—an *ambiguous* grief because it can be unclear where death begins and when grief becomes appropriate.

When we moved Genevieve into an Alzheimer's unit, the conscientious staff did much to help her settle in and adjust. They became her primary caregivers instead of us. Even when Genevieve had lived at a personal care facility, we provided much of the care for her—giving medications, bathing, and such. But when she moved into a higher level of care, she became the responsibility of someone else and began to orient more to her caregivers than to us.

One day, when we went to pick her up for a visit at our house, she was waiting, with makeup on. Genevieve had worn meager makeup in the past but never quite the way she had it on that day. Thick lipstick covered her mouth, and ruby-red rouge plastered her cheeks. Her nails had been painted—something she had never done in our lifetime. When Sharon told her it was time to go to our house to eat, she looked at the caregiver and asked, "Is it all right to go with her?"

It's a real privilege to be a caregiver. It's not an easy job, but it becomes the focus of the relationship with someone who has Alzheimer's. This person depends on you to take care of him or her and help make decisions. But there comes a day, for almost every son or daughter of an Alzheimer's patient, when your older parent becomes unrecognizable to you and you become unrecognizable to him or her. It is a loss. But again, it's a loss that occurs so gradually that many times we forget to say good-bye. Our parents slip right through our fingers, and we lose the chance to tell them what they meant to us, how we will remember them, or how much we will miss them.

Ambiguous grief is part of the package of Alzheimer's disease. You get support to help you cope with your grief, and you remember that it's good to express your heart as you go through the process of loss. But don't let the chance to say good-bye slip away without providing for the opportunity to give and receive a blessing. We do this for our older parent's sake, of course, but we also do it for our own sakes—to give him or her the chance to express love for us. This necessary component can help us make our way through the grief of caregiving.

The Physical Rigors

Caregiving is a physically and emotionally taxing job. In providing care for a parent with Alzheimer's, you can almost expect to double the load, because there's little chance the older parent can work with you. Therefore, it becomes doubly important that you take good care of yourself.

First, *remember that you're not the first to travel this pathway of caregiving*. It's essential to seek the advice of other families and friends who have cared for someone with the disease. The Alzheimer's Association (1-800-272-3900) can be an invaluable source of information; many communities have local chapters. These organizations can help you understand the challenges of the disease and find services, and they can offer care and support to you as a caregiver.

Second, *don't try to do the job alone*. If you are caring for your older parent at home, look for adult day care on a regular basis so you can get some rest. Also, you need hired caregivers, family members, or friends to relieve you of the stress and physical toll aging can demand. Finally, get some emotional and physical support for yourself. The emotions of grief and loss are physically taxing. Don't be afraid to seek regular checkups from your doctor, counseling from professionals or groups, and support from your family and faith community.

Do This in Remembrance

For years I've participated in the Lord's Supper at our church and never given it much thought. "In remembrance" seemed like a trite phrase that meant we gave Christ his due and remembered his sacrifice for us. That's what I *used* to think. Not any more.

Within the last year I began to feel the emptiness and desperateness that fatigue, emotional stress, and loss can bring to the soul. It wasn't just one thing but a combination. First it was the death of my grandmother from Alzheimer's and the grief of seeing my mother struggle with issues regarding her siblings—issues that seemed impossible to solve. Then it was the loss of our friend Rick Husband aboard the space shuttle Columbia. The war in Iraq brought an unusually high client load we struggled to maintain, always one emotional step behind the need. Finally, the suicide of one of my former students utterly upset me. And in the midst of it all was fulfilling our caregiving responsibility for Genevieve and dealing with the stress of normal everyday life with two teens.

It certainly isn't that my life is bad; indeed, it is not. But the accumulated grief had added up. I had, what we call in my business, grief overload.

This compassion fatigue produced in me a sense of being hypervigilant to struggle against depression and hopelessness. My heart sat on the edge, a place where I felt totally empty and unable to give one more ounce—which is, of course, exactly where Christ wants us to be:

> Praise be to the God and Father of our Lord Jesus Christ, the Father of compassion and the God of all comfort, who comforts us in all our troubles, so that we can comfort those in any trouble with the comfort we ourselves have received from God. For just as the sufferings of Christ flow over into our lives, so also through Christ our comfort overflows.
>
> 2 Corinthians 1:3–5

In his most desperate moment—in Gethsemane—Jesus Christ was worn down to the emotional nub of exhaustion. Then the authorities abused him with total disregard for the law or human decency. Finally, he gave his all as he suffered intensely and gave his life on the cross.

When he told us to celebrate Communion "in remembrance" of him, he wasn't instructing us merely to recall his sacrifice; he was inviting us to join him in the most intimate sufferings of his life. He called us to be a part of the same emptiness, knowing that when we empty ourselves and identify with him, we have hope, not only that Christ sympathizes with us, but also that we will partake with him in the ultimate reward in heaven. We must follow the One who entered into joy—but not until he had first suffered pain. Christ rose into heaven only after he died on the cross.

So today when I participate in the Lord's Supper, it is not so much to confess my sin or remember Christ's redemptive work as it is to join my suffering to Christ's. This suffering brings me closer to the eternal God and puts me in contact with his body and his blood. In short, Communion brings me peace. And that's why it is absolutely essential to me.

When we go through the "grief by inches" that Alzheimer's brings, we find out what it's like to be empty, stripped of control, and exhausted. Out of our desperation we seek God. And for me, this is the greatest spiritual lesson I can offer. I emotionally connect to the living God because I have nothing to give and I am utterly dependent. This is where I meet God—and also where I land in the very place Genevieve lives emotionally.

QUESTIONS FOR CONSIDERATION

1. What and who can provide you the necessary resources in the physical and emotional care of your older parent with dementia or Alzheimer's disease?

2. How can you focus on connecting with the long-term memories you still share with your parent?

3. In what ways can you take care of yourself physically, emotionally, and spiritually throughout this process?

7

Show Me the Money:
Legal and Financial Issues

His master replied, "Well done, good and faithful servant!
You have been faithful with a few things;
I will put you in charge of many things.
Come and share your master's happiness!"
Matthew 25:23

I admit it—it floored me when a woman described a problem she was having with a caregiving situation. Although this faithful daughter was providing most of the necessary care for her wealthy mother, her brother was attempting to take total control of the mother's assets.

"I really do worry about how my brother handles my mother's money," she said. "I worry that he'll take it all for himself after she's gone or that she won't have the money she needs for her care. But I just let that go most of the time; it's only money."

I bit my lip and kept my thoughts to myself: *Yeah, it's only money. But I'm not sure I would have the ability to let that much money go!*

Money, estates, and legal issues can cause much of the headache involved in the job of caregiving. Like most people of faith, I believe the words of Jesus about getting too involved with the things of this world: "No one can serve two masters. Either he will hate the one and love the other, or he will be devoted to the one and despise the other. You cannot serve both God and Money" (Matthew 6:24). Paul's words also ricochet around in my head: "For the love of money is a root of all kinds of evil. Some people, eager for money, have wandered from the faith and pierced themselves with many griefs" (1 Timothy 6:10).

Indeed, it is only money. And it does not encompass either the most temporary values in life or the ultimate value at the end of life. So why is it we worry so much about our parent's financial well-being, decisions concerning legal matters, and what will happen to his or her estate after his or her death? Is it only my selfish sinful nature that refuses to let go of its love of money?

Certainly part of me finds it difficult to "let it go," but I doubt the complete answer can be found in my sinful nature. Yes, we are to steer clear of seeking wealth and worshiping money, but we do have a responsibility to take care of practical physical needs here on earth. Paul made this responsibility just as clear as he did the one about avoiding the love of money:

> In the name of the Lord Jesus Christ, we command you, brothers, to keep away from every brother who is idle and does not live according to the teaching you received from us. For you yourselves know how you ought to follow our example. We were not idle when we were with you, nor did we eat anyone's food without paying for it. On the contrary, we worked night and day, laboring and toiling so that we would not be a burden to any of you. We did this, not because we do not have the right to such help, but in order to make ourselves a model for you to follow.
>
> 2 Thessalonians 3:6–9

Clearly, we are to take care of our business while we toil on earth. Jesus also taught this in the parable of the talents (see Matthew 25:14–30). We are responsible to put to good use the things God has entrusted to us. We are to avoid the love of money, even as we are required to make wise decisions about the finances in our control. For caregivers like us, the question is not whether we will have to deal with these financial issues and be part of monetary decision making; it is whether we will be *trustworthy servants* in the execution of our responsibilities.

CONTROL OF FINANCES AND FISCAL DECISIONS

Many of us will have caregiving responsibilities for older parents who are perfectly capable of managing their own finances and legal matters. Even if our older parents have some impairments and cannot manage all of their affairs, many will retain the ability to give overall financial guidance.

As the physical caregiving needs of an older parent increase, however, his or her need to receive assistance with financial and legal matters will typically increase as well. It's wise, then, not only to have the crucial knowledge you need to accept such a responsibility, but also to know how to proceed practically.

Most caregivers struggle first with the issue of whether financial and legal issues are any of their business. Many assume they'll discover the older parent's wishes when he or she dies or becomes totally incapacitated. The problem with this type of reasoning, of course, is that many decisions about an older person's affairs must be made *before* he or she dies or becomes incapacitated.

If you are the primary caregiver to an older parent—no matter what level of care you provide—or are likely to become the primary caregiver, it is *your* responsibility to broach this subject. It *is* your business because it's likely to become your responsibility.

The second issue likely to arise regarding your parent's financial management and decision-making ability centers around his or her desire to remain in control. This is as it should be, because your parent should fulfill his or her responsibilities for as long as possible. As mentioned in the previous chapter, however, a gradualness of decline in the parent must be balanced with the gradient of care. When you see bills going unpaid, regular overdrafts, and an inability to keep accounts responsibly, it's time to take action. In any generation it's a touchy subject to help with or take control of a parent's finances, but the current generation of older people seems particularly sensitive to this issue. As decline becomes obvious and the need more apparent, you must gently ease your older parent toward allowing you to become involved.

You can edge your parent toward this help in many wise ways. It's almost always preferable to offer to help find important papers or to assist in going over confusing financial statements rather than simply taking control. I usually suggest to caregivers that they bring up the subject and connect it with death. I once suggested a man approach his mother by saying something like, "Mom, I know this is a hard subject, but you and I both know that someday you will pass away. I don't know if you've made all the necessary plans or if you could use some help, but I at least need to know what to do with your money and your possessions after you die. If I'm going to be responsible, I want to make sure I know what you would want me to do."

It's hard to say something like this to a parent with whom you've never had a conversation about financial or legal affairs (and it's no easier for the parent to hear), but it does plow the ground necessary to begin the dialogue. In the case above, the mother had made a few plans for funeral arrangements, but the conversation opened the door for the son to ask follow-up statements such as, "If you begin to need care and can't make your own decisions, how do you want me to use your money? If you are in the hospital and are very ill, do you want to be kept alive by machines? If you want me to make some decisions you can't make for yourself, we'll have to find out what needs to be done legally."

Many caregivers hesitate to bring up issues of financial management and decision making because they don't want their parents to think they're after the money. Most caregivers do the job because they care, not to gain some kind of financial reward. Still, it's wise to take stock of your own motives and heed the Bible's warning about the love of money. In my practice and in this generation, I see more and more people who worry about how much money will be left in the estate for themselves after a parent's death rather than being genuinely concerned to help and provide care.

None of us escape this temptation. It may be you were counting on financial help to pay for a child's college education or to get out of debt. It's better to realize this is a genuine temptation—and then to face it rather than to deny it. Ask yourself, "Am I willing to let any financial adviser, lawyer, family member, or friend look at the help or management I'm giving on behalf of my parent's financial planning, estate, or will?" If you're not willing, it may indicate you're not acting in your parent's best interest; you may even be acting unethically.

A coming wave of prosecution in the United States relates to what is called fiduciary abuse. Elder abuse laws have been on the books for years, with mandatory reporting requirements to Adult Protective Services for abuse—and even just suspicion of abuse. These laws most often include not only neglect and physical and emotional abuse but also misuse of an elderly person's assets. You don't want to find yourself defending in court your questionable management or use of your parent's assets.

MAKING A PLAN

If you judge your motives to be clean and your older parent needs help, it's time to develop a plan. Planning will fall into two broad categories: a care plan and an estate plan. Most older people in need of caregiving had no idea they would live as long as they have, nor did they have an inkling of how expensive care would be. Wherever possible, get your older parent involved in the decision-making process; but you'll probably have to take the initiative to begin the process of acquiring information and making decisions.

Wishes and Goals

You'll first want to get a realistic idea of your parent's wishes and goals. Does he or she want to pass on most of the estate to children or family? Do they want to use the available resources for care? Do they want to stay in an independent living situation, or do they prefer assisted living? I find most older parents have some idea of how they want money to be spent—but some can be very apathetic or locked in denial. You must be willing to persevere in the process, in much the same way we described earlier for dealing with a parent's housing situation.

The primary purpose is to decide on a care plan and an estate plan. The care plan should include contingencies for care

- *if your parent stays in his or her current condition,* dealing with such questions as, Is the older parent safe? Is he or she happy with the care received? Are there resources available to maintain the current level of care for the estimated time he or she will live?

- *if your parent should worsen and need substantially more care*, including long-term care, dealing with such questions as, What kind of care would the older parent desire? What kind of care am I willing to provide? Are there resources available to secure long-term care? How will long-term care be provided if needed?
- *if your parent becomes incapacitated and cannot make independent decisions*, dealing with such questions as, Does my parent want to have extraordinary means used to be kept alive? Does my parent want to be resuscitated? Are resources available to provide the care if he or she is totally incapacitated and dependent?

The estate plan should include management of the financial resources to pay for the care plan and details about how the estate will be handled after your parent's death.

In some cases, your older parent may not be physically or cognitively able to give direction. Although this is far from preferable, you as a caregiver may have to work with family members to piece together past conversations to come up with a reasonable plan.

Income and Expenses

After getting some idea of your parent's goals, you need to get a realistic picture of his or her income and resources. Income first includes any monthly Social Security checks, pension checks, or, in rare cases, wages earned. Then you should account for any money available through retirement plans such as a 401(k), an Individual Retirement Account, or Certificates of Deposit. Also, any assets such as equity in real estate and property, stocks, bonds or other investments should be included. Finally, get an accurate account of how much cash is available in savings and checking accounts.

Next, what about expenses? There's something of a safety net during the middle-aged period of life, when you are a working resource. If you get out of straits financially, you can always pick up some extra income through side jobs or second jobs. You also have plenty of time to reverse declining financial fortunes in investments during an economic downturn. But most older people are on a fixed income, meaning their earning potential and investment history is fairly well set. As older persons age, the more needs they'll have and the more of their resources they'll use. Also realize that any inflation in the goods or services your older parent uses will outpace any modest growth of your parent's income. You and your older parent may be particularly blessed, and the care he or she needs may stay the same for a good part of his or her life. But you must be willing to consider how expenses for your elder will dramatically increase if he or she begins to need more help and requires a higher level care; and you're going to have to consider how total incapacitation will be handled as well.

In today's market, expenses can run quite high. It's not unusual for older people to have medication expenses in excess of $800 per month—not to mention any care your older parent may need that can't be provided by the family. If he or she needs some type of home health care from a care aide or health care professional, those costs can easily exceed $100 a day. For an unlicensed, low-level service living facility that provides meals, costs can run from $1,200 to $2,500 per month, depending on amenities. For licensed assisted living facilities with care aides and health care supervision, monthly costs will range from $2,000 to $3,500. Finally, for long-term care in a nursing facility, monthly costs will range from $3,500 to $5,000.

You can see how wise it is to help your parent plan for his or her needs in the future. If your parent's income and assets will not cover expenses, money for care will have to come from somewhere—and that "somewhere" may be from *you*. Certainly, many of us are willing to do whatever is necessary to care for our parents, but expenses can easily affect your own retirement and future care and your own ability to provide education and resources for your children. We're talking about your parent's financial well-being, but we also have in mind the rest of the family.

HELP AVAILABLE: MEDICARE, MEDICAID, AND OTHER INSURANCE

Medicare is a federal government insurance program; for our interests, it services people who are sixty-five and older. If your older parent receives any Social Security, he or she automatically gets a Medicare card. If your parent has never received Social Security, and if for some reason he or she hasn't already applied for and received a Medicare card, you can help him or her do so through the Social Security Administration. There are certain enrollment periods, so it's important to meet these enrollment deadlines.

In a nutshell, Medicare consists of Part A and Part B. Enrollment in Part A is required; essentially it covers most of your older parent's hospital bill in the event that he or she is hospitalized. Though modifications in the plan come from time to time, it will cover basic hospital stays with a semiprivate room, meals, nursing services, supplies, and general hospital services. It will also cover a semiprivate room in a skilled nursing facility for rehabilitation after a hospital stay. In addition, Medicare Part A covers some home part-time nursing care, various rehabilitative therapies, and some medical equipment such as wheelchairs, hospital beds, and walkers. Finally, it covers medical services supplied by a Medicare-approved hospice not otherwise covered in the above parts of Medicare.

Premiums for Medicare Part A are deducted from the Social Security payment each month. Like any insurance program, Medicare Part A has deductibles your older parent must pay for certain services or supplies. (Because Medicare rules can and often do change, it's best to contact Medicare directly each year to keep current with all the latest changes.)

Medicare Part B covers expenses incurred from doctors, laboratories, outpatient services, and supplies. Under some conditions, Part B also covers some home health care services. Currently, your older parent pays a deductible each year and then is responsible for 20 percent of all expenses. While this may be reasonable, the 20 percent figure represents a significant amount in today's health care environment. In order to cover this 20 percent, many people opt for a Medigap policy, which is a health insurance policy sold by private insurance companies to fill the "gaps" in Plan B coverage. Generally speaking, the more comprehensive the coverage and the smaller the deductible, the more the premium will cost. The federal government and Medicare have a list of reputable companies that offer Medigap policies. Investigate each policy well and look for the conditions it covers, preexisting illness clauses, qualification requirements, and any waiting periods. Almost all Medigap policies have overlap clauses, so it's wise to purchase only one.

Almost all older parents who need some level of care are in both Medicare Part A and Part B, unless he or she has another medical insurance plan as part of a retirement package. Note, though, that your parent can join a managed care organization, or HMO. Generally, managed care organizations receive a set amount of money from the government to provide care for enrollees. The organization then provides care and services within its approved network of providers—you must go only to these approved providers to get the maximum coverage. A managed care organization makes money if the services it provides do not exceed the funds it receives from the government.

Recent changes in Medicare now make available a prescription drug benefit. Because the program is new, it's not known whether the program will pick up a significant portion of the costs. Critics believe it won't offer much in the way of coverage, while offering more earning potential to drug companies. Unless your older parent is currently receiving some other prescription drug benefit, however, he or she is likely to benefit from this change.

Anyone who deals with large insurance programs will invariably run into disputes about payments. You must be willing to help your older parent work through these disputes, usually through an appeal process set up through Medicare or a particular HMO. Participating in this appeal process can mean the difference in owing thousands of dollars, so it's an important process to utilize.

Medicaid is an insurance program designed for the benefit of people who live in poverty. This program is run by each state, although both the state and the federal government foot the bill. If your older parent is below the poverty line, you'll need to be ready to help him or her contact the local welfare office, since services and rules often differ from state to state. Generally, if your older parent qualifies for Medicaid, he or she isn't required to pay any premiums or deductibles. Hospitals have to accept Medicaid, but doctors do not. Therefore, you must find doctors who are willing to accept reimbursement from Medicaid.

One major difference between Medicaid and Medicare is that Medicaid covers all prescriptions—usually generic—and doctors' visits. Medicaid also provides payment for services received in some assisted living facilities or long-term care facilities, while Medicare does not provide payment for long-term care (many mistakenly believe it does, and they later discover the bad news when their older parents have a long-term need).

In terms of qualifying for Medicaid, your older parent's home, personal belongings and household goods, and cash value of life insurance policies up to a set amount cannot be counted by the local welfare office. Since the cost of long-term care is enormous, many older people choose to enter a facility and pay for it themselves, eventually spending all their assets; at this point they may qualify for Medicaid.

Some people believe they can put their parent's assets into their names, and thereby qualify the parent for Medicaid. But the government examines qualifying standards for Medicaid with great rigor and will count any assets transferred within the last three to five years as still belonging to your parent. Think carefully before you try a clever strategy to preserve your parent's assets, as the government may consider it fraud and, in some cases, proceed to prosecution. Your parent may "gift" a certain part of his or her assets each year to children and spouses of children. This current allowable gift is $11,000 a year, and it's a good option for the older parent whose goal is to pass along some assets to his or her family.

Long-term care insurance has appeared on the scene only recently. These policies provide payment for some costs associated with long-term care. Again, the more coverage the policy offers, the greater will be the expense to purchase this insurance. It's best to buy a policy when young or middle-aged, since premiums will be much less. In some cases, however, the cost of premiums will dip below the cost of long-term care. It's a good option to pursue if you think nursing home care is a strong possibility for yourself or your older parent. My mother's family, for example, has a strong propensity to live past the age of eighty-five and to develop Alzheimer's in their late eighties. Even though my mother was in her late sixties and the insurance premiums were significant, it made sense to purchase a long-term care policy for her.

THE POWER NECESSARY TO MAKE IT SO

A couple of mechanisms give you the legal power to make financial, health care, and other important decisions on your parent's behalf. The first is called *guardianship*. In guardianship, the court must decree that your older parent is incompetent to handle his or her affairs. The decree will set into motion the appointing of a person to act as guardian, sometimes called a managing conservator. Although the state laws governing guardianship vary, the primary idea is to authorize someone to manage some or all of the older person's affairs, just as if he or she had no decision-making ability. While this may sound like a drastic step, it's necessary in cases where parental deterioration comes suddenly or profoundly and where no previous plans have been made. Since guardianship is a legal decree, an attorney must draft a petition to the court, and your parent will have to be evaluated. Whoever is appointed guardian by the court has the total legal responsibility, just as someone would for a child. If you are appointed guardian, you cannot pass off the responsibility to another sibling or caregiver—unless the court so decrees.

In most cases, a much more reasonable option is *power of attorney*. Power of attorney allows you to make decisions and act on your parent's behalf in doing business—being able to handle all banking accounts, buying or selling real estate, and purchasing or selling stocks or bonds, for example. There are three basic types of power of attorney:

- general power of attorney, which grants rights to act in the name of your older parent on certain issues or for a certain period of time;

- springing, or trigger, power of attorney, which allows you to act in the name of your older parent once a "trigger" occurs, such as your parent becoming hospitalized or diagnosed with Alzheimer's; and
- durable power of attorney, which allows you to conduct business on your older parent's behalf with no ending date.

In my opinion, the best instrument to help your older parent is a durable power of attorney. Both the general power of attorney and the springing power of attorney allow you to act in your parent's name but sometimes offer complications in that some businesses or companies will demand additional documentation to verify the condition or wishes of your older parent. Since this is such an important issue, I believe it's worth hiring an attorney to help you and your older parent draft the power of attorney, making sure the document is done right and providing the necessary support in case questions arise. Be aware that your parent has the ability to revoke a power of attorney or even change the person who holds it. Again, be cautious of other caregivers who may try to get him or her to sign such a document.

Although the power of attorney should allow you to conduct business, it's wise for you and your older parent to pave the way for conducting that business more smoothly. It is a good thing to have your name placed alongside your parent's name on all his or her bank accounts. Any stocks and bonds, life insurance companies, and financial holdings should be given a certified copy of the power of attorney, along with a letter signed by your parent stating his or her wishes. These actions will help you and your older parent make the necessary decisions and take action with the least amount of additional verification or hassle.

Some older people choose to put their assets in a trust—sometimes to reduce estate taxes and sometimes to bypass probate with particular assets. If your parent has set up or wants to set up a trust, a trustee is required. In most instances, the older parent is the trustee, and provisions for a secondary trustee kick in if the trustee dies or becomes incapacitated. As caregiver, you should be identified as a secondary trustee. At the point where your parent needs caregiving, he or she (if able) should have an attorney draft and notarize a letter stating that he or she resigns as trustee and wants the secondary trustee to manage the trust. Technically, the power of attorney instrument should allow you to act on your parent's behalf as trustee, but making the change of trustee is much easier when actually dealing with holdings of the trust.

These documents are very important and should be carefully crafted by an attorney. The National Academy of Elder Law Attorneys (1-520-881-4005) can help you locate an attorney in your area that specializes in elder law. Hiring an attorney is expensive, but it's well worth the expense to avoid legal problems and challenges down the road.

MEDICAL DECISIONS AND ADVANCE DIRECTIVES

Advance directives specify a person's wishes regarding the right to refuse treatment and the appointing of someone to make medical decisions on a person's behalf should he or she become incapacitated. The two types of advance directives are (1) a living will and (2) durable health care power of attorney, or health care proxy. The living will is a legal document in which your older parent indicates the kind of medical interventions and treatments he or she wants or doesn't want used, should he or she be terminally ill, seriously injured, or unconscious or incapacitated and unable to make decisions. It's important to carefully research the requirements of your particular state, or you may want to consider having an attorney draft the living will.

A durable health care power of attorney, or health care proxy, is also a legal instrument that appoints a caregiver or another trustworthy person to make health care decisions if your older parent becomes incapacitated. Although some of these instruments state specifically the types of treatments and interventions desired, the situations that may incapacitate your older parent are very broad, and the contingencies and treatment options usually become clear only when the problem occurs. Since this is another form of power of attorney, it ought to be drafted by a professional.

Of course, these legal instruments won't do you or your older parent any good if they remain on file at the attorney's office or in a lockbox at home. You'll need to make sure that doctors, health care professionals, assisted living facilities, or long-term care institutions have these documents on file.

As I reflect on the days when I worked at a personal care facility, one of my sadder memories involved a lovely woman who had suffered a massive stroke one night while eating dinner. Laura was rushed to the hospital, where she was immediately placed on life support. Laura had a living will, but it was hidden away with other possessions. Her daughter didn't know where it was, nor did she have durable health care power of attorney. Laura lost consciousness and had no hope of recovery, but treatment in the first two days after the stroke kept her alive in the hospital for twenty more days. She did not move, nor did she respond. She lingered while her family suffered, and her resources were drained on care that did her no good. Only after the funeral, when her family combed through her belongings, did someone finally locate the living will that clearly stated her informed consent to refuse care in that very situation.

Make sure you have the necessary documentation readily available to avoid such tragedies.

WILLS

No doubt you've heard the saying hundreds of times—"You can't take it with you." God has decreed that each of us must die, just as he told Adam: "for dust you are and to dust you will return" (Genesis 3:19; see also Hebrews 9:27). We do not create wills because we are tied to money; we create wills because we need to be good stewards who use the resources God has given us in a trustworthy way. If you or your older parent dies without a will, the state in which you live will be forced to deal with the estate—which will often use up a significant portion of the estate and distribute the remainder in ways that sometimes don't make sense.

I often hear older people say something like, "I don't want to make those decisions about who gets what because it will make people unhappy and cause fights." On the contrary, it's exactly when older people do *not* express their wishes that the family often goes to war. Such was the case with a family I met just before the father died.

The large family had six adult children. Their mother had died five years before. Over time the father, eighty-eight-year-old Red, needed more and more care. He had spent his life working at various unskilled jobs in the oil fields of West Texas, and he and his wife had lived on three acres out in the country. The children had been struggling with issues about who would care for Red and how he was to be cared for when he suddenly died of a heart attack.

Red had so little money and belongings by the time he died, it seemed hardly worth making an issue over any of it. Yet, because Red died without a will, the adult children almost came to blows over their parent's possessions and meager resources. The state sold and divided the property, but the possessions continued to be a source of continuous and long-standing fights. It seemed every object—from old eyeglasses to worthless tables and chairs—became a point of contention. I could offer no help. They left my office furious, vowing to never speak to one another again. To my knowledge, they never did.

And here's the real shocker: *All but one of these adult children were confessing Christians*.

How do Christian people take such damaging and drastic actions? Often they do so because a parent's legacy is so important. The legacy reminds us of who we were and therefore suggests who we are. A dead parent's belongings and money cause more contention and bitterness among adult children than any other issue I can think of. Having a will is at least one way of following the Hebrews 12:15 command: "See to it that no one misses the grace of God and that no bitter root grows up to cause trouble and defile many."

Wills do two basic things: (1) they appoint an executor who will be responsible for probating the will, and (2) they specify how the estate should be divided. The executor, upon the parent's death, will take the will, the death certificate, and some kind of personal identification to a local county office. Some states call this probate; others call it probate court. The purpose is to have the executor recognized as the person authorized to carry out various obligations. The executor will inventory all of the assets, arrange to have all debts paid, settle any outstanding claims, pay any taxes, distribute the assets as directed, and then close all accounts. It is demanding work that takes a substantial amount of time. Not only must the executor handle the business, he or she must also be able to handle all the emotions and the relational issues that may exist among family members.

In my opinion, wills should be drafted by attorneys, although some states will recognize handwritten wills. Anyone has the power to change his or her will at any time up until death, as long as he or she has the capacity to know what is being done. Most good wills specify how the major assets should be divided. This includes cash, property, investments, and the like. In addition, many wills state specifics as to personal belongings, such as who gets Mother's jewelry or who gets Dad's valuable coin collection. But for the most part, personal belongings will have to be divided outside of the specifications in the will.

As caregiver, it's your responsibility to make sure your parent has a good, sound will. Not only will it be good for your older parent; it will take care of many future headaches for you as well. In addition, it's important that you help your parent give directions about or begin to let go of personal belongings. If you choose to avoid this important subject while your parent is living, emotional upset will likely result after your parent has passed on.

When your older parent begins to need more care, he or she can lose much of the ability to enjoy "things." The best thing for the older parent is to give away personal possessions while he or she is still living. Not only does this settle the issue, it can be a wonderful opportunity for him or her to connect with significant relationships and to leave a wonderful legacy.

A seventy-eight-year-old woman named Imagine intentionally identified as many objects in her home as possible to give away before she died of cancer. When she gave away an object, she also gave away a story. For instance, she had a nice but fairly beat-up dresser. When she gave the dresser to her grandson, she explained how her husband had made it, and that it was the very first piece of furniture in their home when they got married. In this way, an old dresser suddenly became a prized and sentimental possession. By the time Imagine died, almost everything she owned had been distributed. There was nothing for her family to question.

A less preferable option is to attach to the will a listing of how personal possessions are to be distributed. This list will give the executor and the rest of the family a picture of how the older person wanted things distributed. The list should be fair and straightforward. If you are the executor and caregiver, encourage siblings and family to express their desires for particular possessions or keepsakes. In my family, my father has a gold piece and a rifle that my two brothers connect with Dad. These are sentimental possessions to both and thus have the potential to become points of contention. My father wisely designated in an attachment to his will that one would get the gold piece and the other would receive the rifle.

If this feels like "buzzards circling" and waiting to claim possessions, you're missing the point. It is an effective way to distribute property in a trustworthy way and to avoid roots of bitterness. In one family I know of, the father remarried after his first wife had died. He lived with his second wife for twenty years and then passed away. Although he had tried to give away many of his prized possessions to his children (by his first wife) when he was alive, they resisted; the thought had made them uncomfortable. After he died, however, his wife now rightly owned the possessions. She gave them all— every prized book, china from the first marriage, war decorations—to *her* children. It was certainly not what the father had intended, and it left his children heartbroken.

The methods suggested here place the responsibility of handling the legacy where it rightly belongs—with the older parent. If family members don't like how the distribution is being handled, their issue also rightly remains where it belongs— with the older parent. If the older parent did not leave any directions or gave only partial directions, however, it will be necessary for the executor to divide personal belongings. One tried-and-true method calls for all the immediate heirs to gather at one time for the purpose of dividing the possessions.

In the case of one family, four adult children were each given a sheet of different colored stickers. In sequence from oldest to youngest, each adult child would choose an object he or she wanted by placing a sticker on the possession. This continued in turn until all the possessions had been tagged. Certainly not everyone ended up being totally happy, but everyone agreed that the process had been fair. It's the essential element in trustworthiness—the ability to achieve fairness and justice.

HERE WE GO AGAIN

On occasion my family travels to Europe. On one trip we enjoyed the sights of Rome. Although we didn't find driving to and around Rome a terribly difficult task, driving to our hotel became a big challenge. We weren't exactly lost; we knew where the hotel was located. Yet the one-way streets always seemed to run in the wrong directions for us to get the car to the correct location. As a result, we circled around the same area five or six times.

On our circular journeys we often passed the Coliseum. Although it struck us as spectacular and beautiful upon that first night sighting, it began to look hilarious as we circled by it time and again. Each time we would inch closer to our hotel but without quite making it.

"Here we go again! Let's go see the Coliseum!" we would all laugh. It's the only thing we could do until we finally succeeded in reaching our temporary home.

Dealing with an older parent's financial and legal decisions can feel much the same way. You may not feel lost; you may know exactly what is required. The problem lies in being able to get to where you know you have to be.

These issues take time and a willingness to be persistent. You may not get the whole job done each time you bring up the issues of finances, medical decisions, or wills. You may have to circle around the subjects again and again. You may encounter resistance from your older parent. You may have siblings or family members who disagree with your strategy. But you must realize that if you don't get to the hotel, you'll end up sleeping in the cold. So keep at it.

God has given you the responsibility to not only give love and care but also to use available resources in a trustworthy way. Don't be like the servant in Jesus' parable of the talents. Don't bury your talent in the ground for fear of offending your older parent or upsetting a sibling. Be the servant who will keep nudging your parent on these issues and circling the problems until they finally get solved. You may not be appreciated by your family or even by your older parent for your work. But I do know you'll stand one day before the heavenly Father, assured that you behaved in a trustworthy fashion. And I'm convinced you'll hear him say, "Well done, good and faithful servant!"

QUESTIONS FOR CONSIDERATION

1. Do you know your older parent's wishes concerning their assets, care, and possessions? If not, begin the conversation now.

2. What legal mechanisms do you need in order to be able to supply the care needed and make the necessary decisions should your parent become totally incapacitated or dependent?

3. What possessions are likely to cause squabbles among your siblings or other family members? Encourage your older parent to give these objects to a designated person.

8

The Struggle
of Family Relationships

"My son," the father said, "you are always with me,
and everything I have is yours."
Luke 15:31

Most of us are familiar with the story of the prodigal son and
how he disrespected his father and demanded his inheritance
so he could waste it on a life of debauchery. When the money
ran out and he had nothing to eat, he finally came to his
senses and headed home to work for his old man.

The story beautifully illustrates God's love and grace for
each of us when we finally repent. Jesus runs out in the road
to greet us and rejoices that we have returned to the fold. Most
of us relate to this story because we've played the part of the
rebellious and self-centered prodigal.

But a few of us know all too well the "other" son in the
parable—the older son, who had remained faithful and loyal
to his father, doing just what the father said and making sure
he kept the home place in good repair. After a hard day's
work, he headed back to the house, only to hear the "good
news" that baby brother had crawled back to town and his
father had killed the fattened calf for a "welcome home" feast.

The incredulous brother confronted his father, with words that went something like this: "I've been a good son! *I've* been the one who's been here through thick and thin, making sure everything was taken care of without asking what was in it for me. Now, after squandering the family fortune, this son of yours is ready to come back. And you give him a feast? Where's *my* feast? Where is the fairness?"

If you have been a caregiver for any length of time, no doubt you have some sympathy for the older brother. Maybe none of your siblings have squandered anything; in fact, they may have done nothing wrong at all. But if you've been in the battle for a long time, chances are you've felt that while everyone else's life has moved on, you've been left holding the caregiving bag. A few families have a wonderful mix of orchestrated caregiving, where each family member plays together well and performs competently when it comes his or her time to "solo." But very few families have such a happy situation. Most of us in the breach, who try to hold the dam of life together as we care for our older parents and manage our own lives, will feel the question pop out of our brains from time to time: *Where is the fairness?*

Caregiving for older people simply has not been built into our mentalities. Our society accepts and allows for the care of children; this focus fits well into our lives developmentally. But a tidal wave of change has shifted the landscape of our families in the last half century as the average American's life span has steadily increased. The issue of aging and caregiving is a huge challenge in our society because the family structure necessary to provide such care has yet to develop. We have yet to figure out how to fill the vacuum of needed care and have been unable to implement the necessary generational shifts that caregiving requires.

WHAT IF CAREGIVING WAS NEEDED
AND NO ONE SHOWED UP?

Over the last two hundred years, a natural flow within families has developed in our culture. At times family members must be close; at times they must remain more distant.

When we first marry, we want to draw as close as we can to our spouse to share the intimacy. When children are born, we move even closer to one another to supply the needs of the babies, as well as to provide emotional nurture and protection. The demands of the family require its members to grow very close. But as children grow and become more independent, they must have more freedom and responsibility, which in turn forces parents to pull back. When children reach adolescence, they begin to develop adult identity and start demanding—most of the time in a nice way—that they make their own decisions and choose their directions, occupations, and spouses. Eventually they leave home, marry, and have children of their own. In order for this to happen, a natural rhythm requires parents to pull back and become more distant so their children can learn what it's like to be themselves. This certainly doesn't mean family members don't love one another; it simply means that at various times or seasons the family grows more distant.

When life span averaged sixty-five years, aging people would normally remain fairly vital and active until they suffered a relatively brief terminal illness or injury. The majority of the "elderly" died at an age we'd call young, and, for the most part, extended families had little or no caregiving requirements. Sure, my sixty-five-year-old grandparents cared about me and my parents, but the family had reached a natural time when my parents had to pull closer to me and more distant from their parents. In this world of sixty-five years ago, I may have loved my parents, but our interactions and dependence on one another gradually lessened as I aged.

As life span increased, however, older people suffered much more infirmity that demanded caregiving. This need comes at a time when the natural flow of life has us more distant from our family of origins and more focused on our spouses and children. Just at the time the family in which we grew up needs to draw closer to care for older parents, it's moving further apart. It's really no one's fault; it's simply another adjustment society must make to accommodate the new rhythms of life.

The problem is, of course, that most of us have not made the adjustment.

I love my brothers and my parents, but with a wife and two adolescents to look after, I see the family I grew up in as largely having done its job. I have a brother who lives 350 miles away in another state and another who lives 500 miles away. If my parents develop significant needs for caregiving, will all of us move back in time to a place where we give our family of origin all of our attention? My parents may have needs that demand we stay close at the very time we are all geographically distant.

Laurie, a sixty-year-old retired schoolteacher, discovered this very thing. She recently started caring for her eighty-year-old mother, who had suffered a stroke. "It's not so much that I mind caring for my mother," Laurie says, "it's how the whole thing was dumped on me. I have a younger brother and two younger sisters. They all assumed it was my job to take care of Mother, and they offered to do very little in the way of help. And then they have the gall to give me advice and tell me what I'm doing wrong! I've just about had it! I have a husband, two children, and five grandchildren. I have a lot of things I'd rather be doing than caregiving—especially if I'm not getting any help or appreciation."

Some siblings with older parents live within a reasonable distance of one another and split the care and stress equitably. But it's not the norm for most of us. Most of us are like Laurie and her siblings, who struggle with the needs of our older parents. Who is going to do the job of caregiving? Although I certainly don't pretend to have all the answers—and I'd never suggest that my answers fit everyone—I've come to a couple of conclusions that seem to fit most people.

One Primary Caregiver, One Primary Caregiving Group

I view the job of caregiving as a race. We all once ran the race with our mother, father, and siblings in a cooperative effort. But along the way, we and our siblings started peeling off to different tracks and courses that took us to our current families and further and further away from the original race. We left the former race of life to our parents and trusted they'd be able to finish their course as we pressed on with our own lives.

But as older parents demonstrate that they can't finish by themselves, someone from the original family must go back to help them get to the finish line. In most cases, it's not feasible for all siblings to go back to the original track. Fair or not, caregiving usually calls for *one* primary caregiver.

Too often, however, this responsibility is not the result of a careful decision but an *assumption*. It typically happens in two ways. First, the family assumes there is one particular sibling who will naturally take on the job of caregiving—even the sibling who is to do the caregiving shares the assumption. Laurie's siblings always believed she would take over the care of their mother because Laurie lived in the same town and was the oldest child. No one ever discussed anything; Laurie simply took the job when her mother was in need of care. Not only is such an assumption unfair; it often leads to tremendous resentments and frustration.

The caregiving job also can be assumed by default. In this case, no one takes on the job of caregiving, and a vacuum forms around the need. In these situations, siblings move slowly, often looking for creative ways to avoid becoming the primary caregiver. The sibling who eventually feels the most responsibility reluctantly assumes the caregiving role. This situation can lead to even more anger and frustration.

Of course, it's best to discuss caregiving with the older parent and siblings long before a need appears. But barring that, the discussion *must* take place when the need becomes apparent. Such communication must occur, not only to ensure that the best caregiving will be provided, but also to work out the details of *who* can best provide the care.

Since Laurie's mother couldn't communicate, I set up a meeting with Laurie and her three siblings to do some necessary backtracking on the caregiving job.

"I thought you *wanted* the job," said Gary, Laurie's brother. "You and Mother have always been so close; I always assumed you two had communicated about it." Laurie's two sisters nodded in agreement.

"Even though it may have been reasonable to assume Laurie would do the caregiving for your mother," I responded, "I always find it helpful for the whole family to talk about all the issues involved with care because it's such a weighty responsibility."

Carrie, the youngest sister, blurted out, "I just have to get this out. I am so nervous about you [Laurie] not doing this. I'm sorry because it *is* such a big job, but I just *can't* do it, and I don't really want to do it either."

Carrie's confession ignited Laurie's anger. "You don't really *want* to do it? What about me? You just leave it to me without any support?"

I interrupted and tried to defuse the tension. "Carrie," I said, "I know it must feel threatening to you to talk about taking care of your mother, but simply saying you can't or won't makes it feel as though Laurie is left to go down with the ship. No matter how much or little you care for your mother, all of you have reasons why caregiving is not convenient or easy. I'd like to hear those reasons." (I always seek to facilitate communication among family members by uncovering the reasons people say they cannot give care. It gives everyone a hearing and usually reveals hidden motives or secrets.)

Laurie went first and expressed her desire to be a grandmother to her grandchildren and to have fun with her family. "I've worked hard, and now's just the time I want to reap some of the precious time with my kids," she declared.

Gary lived hundreds of miles away, and he focused on the responsibilities of his job as an aircraft engineer. Linda, the next oldest daughter, also had job responsibilities, and she was dealing with a drug-addicted son. Carrie focused on a recent trauma in her life. "I know I haven't said anything to any of you," she said, "but my husband and I are about to declare bankruptcy. The kids are in college, we're hopelessly in debt, and it's largely my fault. We're not only in a financial mess, but my husband has threatened to divorce me. I just can't imagine adding the stress of caring for Mom on top of all this." (After uncovering the siblings' concerns and their reasons for avoiding caregiving, I try to move everyone to discuss what they can do to address the need.)

"You all have legitimate concerns and desires for your own lives, which will be affected by the need to care for your mother," I said, "but it's important for you to find out what you're willing and able to do." I sent them back home to discuss with their families what they were willing and able to provide by way of support and care.

In a conference call with the four of them the next week, I discovered that significant progress and discoveries had been made. Gary said he and his wife would be willing to move his mother to their town, but it would require that she stay in a care facility. "I have no idea what Mother's finances are," he said, "but I assume we'd all have to provide some financial support to pay for the care." Linda made a similar offer, but Carrie remained adamant that she couldn't offer any help whatsoever.

Interestingly, Laurie grew much softer after hearing her siblings' responses. "It helps me to hear what all of you are willing to do," she said. She reported that she and her husband discussed doing some of the caregiving in their home but felt they needed "significant" periods of time off from caregiving. She also declared that she had done some work on her mother's finances and didn't think she could afford long-term care unless "we all kicked in significant amounts of money."

I believe one person ought to be the primary caregiver, because the "distant" nature of the aging family does not facilitate good communication and quick decisions. And it's usually the easiest and simplest solution to have one caregiver. But the job of caregiving can become too large for any one person to handle. The primary caregiver needs a *primary caregiving unit*. In Laurie's case, the caregiving unit consisted of her and her husband. The caregiving responsibility was often going to fall to her husband, compelling him to significantly change his lifestyle. But the caregiving unit also needs support from community and governmental services and from the other family members. So while the burden of duties falls mostly on the primary caregiver as the point person, everyone in the family has a role to play in the care of the older parent.

By the time my mother-in-law, Genevieve, had suffered a stroke and spent several days in the hospital, the family had discussed the possibility and sequence of care but hadn't resolved many of the specifics. Although Sharon's brother and his wife had expressed a willingness to move Genevieve to a care facility in their town, we decided it would be best for her to stay in the same town and that Sharon would function as the primary caregiver. She would be the primary force in making decisions concerning health care, medical appointments, living arrangements, and managing finances. In order for the operation to work, however, my children and I had to support Sharon's caregiving effort, which meant that I became responsible to keep track of Genevieve's neurological treatment and her medication regimen, to drive her to where she needed to go, and to serve as a sounding board for Sharon in decision making. Our children had to give up time for "just our family" and understand that Genevieve's care would occasionally interfere with their activities. Although we didn't do anywhere near the work Sharon was doing in caregiving, we had crucial roles. If Sharon had to go it alone or continually badger the rest of us to help, it would have drained a significant amount of the energy necessary for caregiving.

But the support couldn't stop there. John, Sharon's brother, took off from work when Genevieve first had the stroke to be with her as we worked out the specifics of her care. Sharon's uncle makes regular calls to express appreciation for her work and to give important advice and direction on finances. Extended family members, such as my parents and John's mother-in-law, also have come to visit, to help where they can, and to take Genevieve to appointments. If Sharon had expected me or John to do work that would equal the care she provides, it would have caused a significant amount of confusion. When Sharon took the role of primary caregiver, she became the point person. *All* family members, however, must function in their roles in order to make things work. Does John have the right to make decisions for his mother? No, unless he takes over the role of primary caregiver. He does, however, have an essential role to play in supporting, talking through decisions, and providing respite for Sharon.

Some families function as "caregivers by committee," with everyone doing an equal share. If this works for your family, then by all means share the load equally. But in this age of families living in different locations and having distant relationships, the model I've described usually works best. Even so, there will always be problems and emotional issues to work out as everyone learns their roles. Sharon and John have had several discussions to iron out issues of care, and it hasn't always been easy. But if the family agrees on the primary caregiver and the roles of all involved, these problems can usually be solved by good communication along the way.

If You Have the Responsibility, You Must Have the Power

Laurie and her siblings decided Laurie would become the primary caregiver of her mother, with the consent and support of Laurie's husband. Gary, Linda, and even Carrie in the end committed themselves to function in support roles. Their communication with each other seemed, for the most part, to keep Laurie's anger from boiling over.

I hadn't seen the family for about a year and a half when I received an urgent call from Gary, requesting that he and siblings come for another meeting. Things had functioned fairly well for about eight months after our original meetings, but then Carrie's bankruptcy and divorce were finalized and she moved back to the town where Laurie lived. She began spending more and more time with her mother, giving Laurie and her husband much-needed breaks. Their mother had improved slightly in her ability to communicate and had settled into a day-to-day routine of living with her daughter.

But eventually Carrie began questioning Laurie's management of the finances. Also, their mother became increasingly angry with Laurie and her husband, although the reasons never seemed clear. A crisis occurred when Carrie presented Laurie with a durable power of attorney, signed by her mother. An angry and hurt Laurie called her brother and other sister, and so they all came to see me.

"I just think I have more time and can do a better job than you," Carrie said to Laurie as we began our meeting. "Besides, I would think you'd be grateful for one less thing to do."

Laurie shot back, "I don't think this has anything to do with giving me more time. I think you just want to get ahold of mother's few resources for yourself!" Gary and Linda nodded in agreement, and their mother watched in agony.

"She's my mother too, and you have no right to think you can make all the decisions!" Carrie responded.

Although the discussion raged back and forth, it became clear that, while Carrie wanted to take over her mother's finances, she had no desire to take over her full-time care. "I think I can do a better job with the money, but I have to work to support my kids during the day," she said.

Since the children remained divided, I chose to address the person in the middle—the mother. Although she had limited speech and clearly was struggling with some dementia, she could understand most of what I said. "I know you love all your children, and it must break your heart to see them fight," I said as the mother nodded.

Then I addressed the children: "There's nothing more difficult than having responsibility but having no power to do what is necessary. Who does what thing best is not really the question here. Carrie, you actually may be better at finances than Laurie, and Laurie may be better at caring for your mother. But the fact is, giving the required care without having the ability to make the necessary financial decisions is like building a house with no materials. So where the financial management goes, the caregiving should follow—and vice versa."

It's not just an issue of family members having different opinions about what's best for their older parents. These conflicts and opinions can be worked out with a renewed commitment to communication and tolerance. But separating power and responsibility is a recipe for disaster. Caregiver, older parent, and family members all lose.

I asked each family member to express his or her opinion about the separation of finances and caregiving. Predictably, only Carrie expressed doubt about the necessity of keeping the two together. I looked at the mother and said, "I know it's difficult, but do you understand that it's best to have the one who takes care of you and the one who pays your bills be the same person?" She nodded her head. "Then it really comes down to who you think would do the best job in doing both." After glancing at Carrie tenderly, she reached over and placed her hand on Laurie's knee and said, "Yes."

It would be nice to say that everything immediately fell into place for the family and the issue got settled. Unfortunately, Carrie stomped out of the meeting, and Laurie had to move quickly to regain the durable power of attorney. Although communication did improve between the sisters over the course of several years, the conflict took its toll on their relationship. But the toll would have been much greater for everyone had the job stayed divided. Laurie would have lacked the funds to care for her mother properly, and Carrie might have abused her mother's resources.

SOME WORDS TO THE WISE
ABOUT FAMILY RELATIONSHIPS AND CAREGIVING

I've seen it happen many times in a variety of family situations. A primary caregiver gives his or her heart and soul in devoted care for the older parent. The older parent, cranky or frustrated by his or her lack of control and ill health, takes it out on the caregiver. While this is bad enough, the older parent then goes out of his or her way to compliment one of the siblings. "I'm so proud of my son," or, "Those children of my daughter are really special and talented," or, "I think I want to send them a gift; go and get them something." These kinds of statements (and many more) have been said to caregivers by their older parents about anyone other than the caregiver—and that's a painful burden to bear for the caregiver.

As a caregiver, it's important to realize your older parent probably isn't intentionally trying to disrespect you or make you angry. Most likely, he or she assumes you know how he or she feels about you. Instead of allowing anger and bitterness to fester, reach beyond yourself and ask a question like, "Mom, you always talk about how pleased you are with my brother; are you pleased with me?" Most of the time this elicits some reassurance from the older parent. But many caregivers say, "If I have to ask for it, it won't mean anything." In painful honesty I have to say to the caregiver, "If a man asks for a fish and gets it, isn't that better than going hungry?" Overwhelmingly, your older parent cares for you and will respond out of love when prompted.

Don't Believe Everything You Hear

If you are the sibling of a primary caregiver, don't be surprised if you get a call from your older parent complaining about your hardworking brother or sister. You will hear how the caregiver is mean, or how he or she is misusing money, or how he or she is giving away all of the furniture—or any number of other issues. Your natural response will be to pick up the phone and call your sibling to ask, "What are you doing? What's going on there?" But just know that when you say these things, you're striking at the heart of the caregiver, who most often is doing the best he or she can do.

When your parent calls you to complain, much of the time it's because he or she is upset at the caregiver and thus is doing what we all do in an argument—trying to get others to take our side! In some cases, the older parent reports something you'd agree was a mistake on the part of the caregiver or describes a situation you may have handled differently. As I've suggested throughout this book, caregiving is a tough job and caregivers make mistakes. But this simply isn't the point. Your caregiving sibling *deserves* your support and care, not only when he or she does things well, but also when he or she falls short. Not everyone in the family can leave their lives to share the load; in the sacrifices they make on behalf of your loved one, the caregiver is entitled to your support. You may want to report to the caregiver what the parent said, but be sure not to accuse or take action until you get the whole story.

I typically tell caregivers to use a simple statement to answer their siblings' accusations or displeasure: "If you don't approve of how I'm handling things, or if you feel you can no longer support me, I'll be more than happy to turn the job over to you." Sometimes caregivers *are* doing an inadequate job, but before you go on the offensive, make sure you're willing to take over the responsibility of caregiving yourself.

Don't Wait for a Crisis

Caregiving is not only a laborious job; it is a lonely job. Often, the meager time extended families spend with one another gets consumed by the issues of caregiving. As a result, caregivers often talk with their siblings only when a crisis or problem arises. This tends, however, to isolate the caregiver and make the siblings dread phone calls or other family contacts.

It's best to schedule times for regular phone calls or visits. Often, few caregiving issues will need to be discussed, and the conversation and visit can focus on deepening the relationship. Sharon made a wise move at the beginning of her mother's care; she asked her brother, John, to plan a visit once a quarter. Even though this hasn't always been possible, the regularity of visits has reduced Sharon's loneliness and the emotional pressure of losing her mother to Alzheimer's disease.

The Worker Deserves the Wages

It is a heartbreaking thing to see at the end of life. The older parent, unwilling or unable to divide his or her possessions, just hopes the children will sort it out after his or her death. The primary caregiver, eager to be scrupulously honest, takes care not to spend one dime more of the parent's money than seems absolutely necessary. The caregiver invests a good portion of his or her life—years, sometimes decades— into the job of caregiving. And finally, when the parent dies, all the possessions and resources get divided equally. Not only does this seem unfair; it leaves the caregiver with a feeling of being undervalued and unappreciated. Sometimes the scars on the family relationships are permanent.

The Bible speaks to this inequity. Paul writes, "For the Scripture says, 'Do not muzzle the ox while it is treading out the grain,' and 'The worker deserves his wages'" (1 Timothy 5:18). Let me be clear: the primary caregiver is entitled to more of the resources and belongings of the older parent because he or she is bearing the heaviest load and doing the work. Interestingly enough, I find it's not the siblings who most often resist this idea but the caregivers themselves. As a caregiver, you must understand that you will respond emotionally to injustice. If you resist being paid and being compensated with some of your parent's possessions, you're setting the stage for future anger and resentment.

The wage must be reasonable, of course, and must be clearly discussed with all siblings. I find, however, that when siblings get clear about the issue and institute the compensation while the caregiving takes place, families usually work together more effectively. Granted, getting compensated for a job you feel should be done only out of love does feel uncomfortable. But the benefit of avoiding injustices and anger in the sibling relationships, in my opinion, far outweighs the negatives.

Watch Out for the Fractures

Despite their best efforts at communication and connection, family members will vigorously disagree on some issues. It may be because the siblings have never gotten along well, or it may be a son or daughter wants something from the older parent that he or she will never get. It may be because they don't see eye to eye on the kind of care the older parent needs. No matter the reason, at times family members will end up on different sides of the fence.

The best that can be hoped for is to remain connected and willing to tolerate a variety of differences. Some issues in aging simply cannot be solved, but if we resist making it a make-or-break situation, we can salvage the relationship. Few things are worth the risk of fracturing a family relationship. Chances are your family relationships will last far longer than your job of caregiving. God tells us, "Be devoted to one another in brotherly love. Honor one another above yourselves" (Romans 12:10). If you can remain connected, even through differences and hard times, you will reap the reward of being part of a close family. Love really does cover over a multitude of problems (see James 5:20; 1 Peter 4:8).

WHERE IS THE FAIRNESS?

Remember the "other" son? He had given a good portion of his life to make sure he managed his responsibilities well so that his father would be proud of him. When his father welcomed back the lost son, we could hear the older son crying out, "Where is the fairness?"

We take on the job of caregiving for a variety of reasons. Some of us do so because we love our parents. Some of us give care out of obedience to the command to honor our fathers and mothers. Some of us take the job because no one else will do it. But no matter the reason, it's highly doubtful you will be paid back in full for all you do for your older parent. No one will be able to make up for lost time with children or grandchildren. No one will be able to cut an appropriate wage check for your endless hours of changing briefs or cleaning soiled clothes. No one will be able to say enough words of appreciation or thankfulness for the days and even years that get cut from your life. You will, most likely, die with a debt owed to you.

Where is the fairness in all this?

"'My son,' the father said, 'you are always with me, and everything I have is yours'" (Luke 15:31). Yes, you will most likely die with the debt unaddressed—but the debt will not be forgotten. The One who cares for us most, who loves us best, and who knows all about debt payment has taken special note of our circumstances. Let's not be hasty in our anger or our judgments about injustices, because Christ himself will give us all that he has in glory. This is enough payment for me, and I believe it's enough payment for all the "other" sons and daughters in the universe of caregiving.

QUESTIONS FOR CONSIDERATION

1. What issues do you see as unfair in your job of caregiving?

2. As a family, who serves in the roles of primary caregiver, primary caregiving group, and supporters of the caregiving effort?

3. How can you facilitate better communication among all family members who have a stake in caregiving?

PART 3

Embracing the Hope of Defeat

Dear friends, do not be surprised at the painful trial you are suffering, as though something strange were happening to you. But rejoice that you participate in the sufferings of Christ, so that you may be overjoyed when his glory is revealed.

1 Peter 4:12–13

Problems, problems, problems. Caregiving is chock-full of problems. But the biggest problem of all is that some problems just cannot be solved. Some issues in caregiving are like walking up an escalator at one mile an hour when it is going down at two. In the end, caregiving is a losing proposition.

Caregiving for an older parent, if done correctly, doesn't result in our parent living on indefinitely. If we succeed, our older parent loses all control, all that was once held as precious, and finally life itself. And when our older parent faces such an ultimate defeat, we face it right along with him or her. So what's the use anyway?

In this defeat we find ultimate victory. Jesus Christ achieved for us this triumph when he willingly suffered the humiliation of becoming human, the ridicule of working in situations where others did not understand, and the sting of death on the cross. In caregiving, defeat joins us with the One who suffered the biggest "defeat" of all. But there we also join his victory over everything that makes our lives difficult. In our defeat, we find our hope.

9

Depression and
the Fall to Nowhere

So my spirit grows faint within me;
my heart within me is dismayed.
Psalm 143:4

All the trite statements in the world ran through my head in what seemed like a moment.

- "Look on the bright side."
- "You have your family to live for."
- "You want to see your grandchildren grow up."
- "All things somehow work together for good."

But none of these platitudes (or the others too numerous to mention) helped me as I sat in the face of such a heavy and downtrodden spirit. Matthew was a seventy-seven-year-old retired banker with leukemia. He had come to the personal care home on his own volition because he knew he was going to need increasing care. But his situation deeply depressed him. He had been married twice—both ending in divorce—and had two children.

"I was pretty hard on my son when he came to work at my bank," he admitted. "We really haven't spoken in years, and I think my daughter checks in on me only out of obligation."

"Any grandchildren?" I asked, hoping to find something positive to set my therapeutic hooks into.

"Yes, I have two," Matthew replied. "No, wait, I think I have three."

It quickly became obvious he had developed as little a relationship with his grandchildren as he had with anyone else in his family. After several minutes of silence as I resisted the pat answers, he looked me straight in the eye and said, "I've spent my life making money. I've been married unsuccessfully twice; I've got two children who don't care for me and I don't really have much connection with them, and I'm in a care facility where all I can expect is to get worse. I've had a wasted life, and I'm going to die all alone."

I felt stunned; he had voiced the very thought I had—one that has struck me many times when someone has said to me, "I have nothing to live for."

I spent a lot of time with Matthew, taking him to appointments, eating lunch with him, taking him to movies, and trying to show him the truth about a relationship with the living God. But Matthew never really made a connection with me (or with anyone else, as far as I knew). His deep depression, like a shroud that wouldn't lift, isolated him from everyone. So it didn't surprise me much when I received a phone call from a care aide informing me that she had found Matthew in his shower with a bullet in his head. He had wasted his life. And he *did* die alone.

DEPRESSION IS NOT "THE BLUES"

Almost everyone has periods of emotional ups and downs. At times we don't feel sharp; we feel cut off or alone or generally sad because of some situation or loss. We sometimes describe these times as being blue, in a funk, or depressed.

But when professionals talk about clinical depression, we have in mind an affective disorder much deeper than these familiar feelings.

Depression has two identifiable aspects. The first is a loss of a feeling of interest or an inability to experience pleasure in normally pleasurable activities. Depressed people often look lifeless, dull, or sad. They describe themselves as "feeling dead" or constantly "having a black cloud" on top of them. A normally involved mother leaves her children to fend for themselves, or a hardworking father who usually loves his job feels overwhelmed with the very idea of work. In other words, the person suffers from a major emotional or affective mood disturbance.

Second, depression affects the biological well-being of the person. Depressed people may have an unintentional weight loss or gain, be unable to sleep (or sometimes they find they sleep almost all the time), feel extremely agitated (or sometimes they have almost no motor activity), have decreased energy, or have diminished sexual interest. Depression affects not only one's mood and emotions but also his or her physiology and behavior.

Depression sometimes gets called the "common cold" of mental health disorders simply because it strikes so many in the general population. But this deep trough is especially common in people aged sixty-five and older. We often think of adolescence as the time in life most at risk for depression and suicide. Think again. Depression is at least *two times* as common among older people than in the general population; at least 25 percent of all suicides committed in the United States occur among the elderly. This suicide rate is especially high among males aged seventy and over. Not only do these older males try suicide more often; they succeed an astonishing 90 percent of the time as compared to just 13 percent of adolescents.

CAUSES OF DEPRESSION

Why is depression so common in the older population? It really isn't so surprising if you look at the overwhelming tasks and stresses that accompany aging.

Psychological Loss

Think of the pileup of losses—retirement from the status of job and career; loss of earning ability, resulting in reduced financial resources; loss of family focus due to adult children having grandchildren of their own; reduction of physical strength, often accompanied by cognitive deterioration; inability to control one's environment, resulting in loss of the house or apartment; inability to maintain self-care; loss of ability to drive; and the deaths of spouse and friends.

Americans seem especially attached to their abilities to control and to remain independent. The number one predictor of happiness and life satisfaction in the older population is not connection with family, or even physical prowess, but independence. Living in my own house, driving my own car, making the decisions of what I want to buy and where I want to be—these are the things that make me satisfied with life as I grow old.

But for those who come to need ongoing care, aging breaks the illusion of control. Aging can be like an artillery barrage on the fortress of our self-sufficiency and independence. As the losses get lobbed into our lives, one wall and stronghold after another fall until the front gate holding back the onslaught of hopelessness has nothing left to hold on to and finally gives way. The question is not, "Why is depression so common among the elderly?" but rather, "Who wouldn't be depressed in the face of such loss?"

Chronic Illness

Depression has many causes beyond the psychological issues of loss. Older people also struggle with physical deterioration and chronic illness. Those who have never been chronically ill find it difficult to understand how accumulated pain and sickness take a toll on one's body.

A few years ago on a visit to see my sister, I took a stroll outside in the woods for a few minutes in the lovely fall weather. After my walk I discovered that my legs were covered with ticks. This infestation led to the Lyme disease that eventually wreaked havoc on my autoimmune system. I speak from experience when I say that chronic illness can rob life of joy and make it very difficult to fight off depression.

Chronic illness does more than discourage a person psychologically. It pounds the body relentlessly until another system of the body is also affected and tries to compensate. This compensation, in turn, affects another system and another— until a person feels worse and worse. The brain also gets pulled into the illness. Day after day of pain or inactivity leaves the brain to use its resources to manage the attack, with little energy left over for intellectual pursuits, relational interactions, or recreational enjoyment. If you can excuse the nonmedical description, chronic illness numbs the brain into submission because of the daily demands of managing stress. Depression is the result and frequent companion of chronic illness.

Being sick or in pain day after day is like a death march. Each day brings a higher level of distress and a decreased chance of recovery. Movement becomes labored, and hope feels impossible to maintain. Certainly the psychological challenge of being sick all the time gets depressing, but remember that the body itself numbs the brain and causes the person to become depressed.

Brain Chemistry and Depression

Even with tremendous advances in brain research, what we don't know still far outweighs what we do know. We can compare brain scans of depressed people with the normal population and see a marked difference in brain activity between the two groups. The brain uses chemical messengers to communicate from one brain cell to the next in producing thoughts and actions, so there's little doubt that a chemical cause explains the difference. But we don't know the cause or process of this chemical activity. In the broadest sense, there are three basic theories that seek to explain how the chemical process brings on depression:

- The primary chemical causing brain cells to activate (serotonin) somehow gets in short supply or goes unproduced. Instead of brain cells actively communicating to one another, no chemical messenger stimulates the cells to "talk" to one another, leaving the person emotionally blunted and flat in activity.
- While brain cells are communicating, or "firing," the process goes unregulated. As a result, brain cells try to communicate at a rapid rate but without good reception. Like a television set with poor reception, the messages get sent, but the cells can't pick them up. The result is a malfunction in brain activity. As brain cells communicate, each cell sends a chemical message to the next brain cell. The part of the chemical message not received by the next brain cell usually gets reabsorbed by the original cell for use in later messages.
- The originating brain cell releases the chemical message, but because of a malfunction in the brain, it reabsorbs the chemical too quickly, thus inhibiting the next brain cell from receiving the message.

These explanations represent current ideas of what happens in the brain chemistry of a depressed person. The problem is, no blood test or cognitive observation can tell physicians exactly which process (or processes) is going on. As a result, we have to surmise the likely causes of chemical imbalances in the brain and then guess at which medications can restore balance.

A Wasted Life

As a person nears death, it's natural for him or her to look back on life to try to make sense of the legacy he or she will leave behind, the people who have been affected, and the good or evil done. We love to picture our aging parent entering the final days of life—with the family gathered around to get sage advice and to look at pictures of joyous times gone by—and slipping into death knowing that all is well. This is an accurate picture for many but certainly not for everyone.

Some, like Matthew, find themselves cut off from their families, saddled with a life filled with nothing but fruitless efforts, having nothing to show for it all but the emotional baggage they'll leave behind. When these older people think about death, they do not feel comforted that all is well; instead, they see life as incomplete and unhappy. Early developmental psychologists rightly called this dark reaction *hopelessness* or *despair*. It's something like stealing a precious object and having a perfect escape plan, only to discover that the object was a counterfeit and that execution awaits as punishment for the crime. You have no enjoyment of genuine accomplishment, and you'll suffer the ultimate consequence for the action.

Many older people get thrown into a depressive episode because of this type of life evaluation. In fact, how the older person has lived and has managed relationships is a matter of record. It is neither an illness to be cured nor a perception that can be changed; the past is reality. Despair and depression often result when the person realizes the truth of the evil done and the emotional trauma that will be left behind. Not only does the older person feel the sorrow of a wasted life; he or she believes nothing can be changed.

TREATING DEPRESSION

Elaine was a seventy-nine-year-old widow with three adult daughters. She felt terribly depressed when she visited my office. Like many older women, she had endured a relentless hammering of losses.

When she was seventy-three, her husband began to have serious heart problems, which forced her into shaping her life around caring for him. When he died three years later, she not only lost her life companion of fifty-seven years but also moved from her home to be in the same town as Katie, her middle daughter. Although she made this move voluntarily, she didn't realize she would be permanently leaving behind all of her friends and familiar surroundings. Now at age seventy-nine she had become debilitated from the arthritis she had suffered with for many years. She moved to my care facility to get the daily assistance she needed in dressing, bathing, and eating.

"I'm just out of gas," she said to me. "There's really no reason for me to live because I don't do anyone any good."

"Mother," objected Katie, "that's not true. You have us and your grandchildren to live for."

Elaine nodded lethargically, but she clearly had no connection to the statement. In Elaine, I was seeing all the tumblers fall into place for major depression. She had experienced tremendous psychological loss of husband, home, and health; was in chronic pain; suffered a chemical rut of depression; and had dedicated her life to her husband and their life together instead of connecting to the families of her children and grand-children.

Dealing with Loss: Remember and Connect

It's a painful truth that loss, one of the primary characteristics of aging, cannot be modified. Close friends and some family members have now died or become infirm in their own old age. The older person often has had to move from a home and familiar surroundings and has lost the ability to work and to care for himself or herself. It's easy for young or middle-aged individuals to forget just how difficult it is to travel this rocky road. We tend to think, *Well, that's just the process of life*, or, *What do you expect? You're old, and this is what happens when you're old*. We want to be sensitive, but we get trapped in our "problem solving/facing reality" mode.

Grief due to loss means something different to older people than it does to younger people. When a younger person experiences a loss, he or she may feel sad but quickly moves on to adapt his or her life around the loss; he or she typically has many other things to concentrate on that can help fill the void. After older people have accumulated a threshold of loss, they simply aren't involved in enough other things to fill the void. Adaptation to the loss, therefore, is not as natural.

Such was the case for Elaine. Her daughter Katie wanted her to live for her three daughters and her grandchildren, but Elaine had never been an essential part of the lives of those families. She felt more connected to her husband, friends, and community than to the everyday lives of her daughters' families.

I typically try to use a couple of different strategies when dealing with a person who is suffering from depression due to loss. The first is to *help him or her remember*. Many younger people who are problem solvers tend to avoid any talk about the loss that has caused the depression. With older people, it's just the opposite. The connection to what they've lost remains an essential emotional pillar for their lives.

"Tell me about your husband—how you two met and how you and he built a life together," I requested of Elaine as I talked with her and Katie.

She offered little. "We met when we were young and got married and lived in Arkansas," she replied. Such short answers typify the responses of depressed older people, but I persisted in my questioning.

"But tell me about how you two met and how he asked you to marry him."

Elaine started slowly but began piecing together the story. "He worked on a dairy farm my parents owned in Arkansas. I always thought he would have an eye for my older sister because he never did pay much mind to me. But I came to find out he was shy around me because he really wanted to be with me."

I sensed she had begun to enter the story, so I said, "So he chose you over your sister? How did he finally get around to asking you to marry him if he was so shy?"

Elaine's flat and distant look started to fade, and she proceeded to tell an engaging story about how her husband courted her, when they first kissed, and how he proposed to her. Although these stories related to the very things she had lost, they connected her with her emotional life and built her energy. Such a connection builds an ability to adapt to loss.

The second strategy in dealing with depression due to loss is to *help the person connect*—to take an emotional connection from a past loss and turn it into connection with present relationships. To encourage this in Elaine, I asked, "How did your husband make you feel special or loved?"

Elaine thought for a couple of minutes and finally said, "He'd always give me a look before he left the house and say, 'Be here later?' I would say yes, and he'd give a little nod and wink. It always made me feel there was no place he'd rather be."

"That is such a beautiful story," I said. "Do you do the same thing with your daughter?"

Elaine answered with a no, saying, "That was always his word."

"I see that," I replied, "but it also makes me think it was his way of teaching you how to make someone else feel special. I wonder if you could make your daughter feel that special."

"I guess I could."

We talked about many other things in the session, but as Katie got up to leave, Elaine held her daughter's hand. Struggling to overcome her flat emotional state, Elaine said, "Be here later?"

Katie's eyes welled up with tears as she responded, "I'll be back later."

Elaine gave her a wink.

Encourage Getting Up and Getting Going

When a person feels depressed, even the simplest of tasks becomes overwhelming. People describe feeling consumed with anxiety at the task of getting dressed, or they may say that it actually hurts to take a shower. If this is hard to understand, try to think of the last time you had the flu or a bad cold. You probably didn't feel like doing much. Depression is a sickness. It attacks the brain and causes dramatic errors in thinking and reasoning.

Unlike the flu, however, getting up and staying on a routine helps to fight off depression. Of course, to the person who suffers from depression, daily tasks can seem impossible, and so caring people must help the person stay active and use his or her brain.

When I suggested to Elaine that it would be good for her to stay on a schedule, she responded reluctantly. "I just don't know if I can do anything," she declared.

"That's why I'm going to ask Katie and my staff to help you stay on track," I replied. "Would you be willing to let us help you stay on schedule?"

"I guess so."

I worked with Katie in establishing a reasonable schedule for her mother that included getting up, getting dressed, eating regular meals, taking a daily walk, and participating in two other daily activities.

"My staff knows this," I said to Katie, "but I want you to be aware that it will be difficult for your mother to do these activities, and she will resist at times. Even when she does participate, you'll most likely notice that she has a blank expression and is uninvolved. It's important for us to press on and have your mom stay on schedule as much as possible—for her sake."

I explained that by receiving regular stimulation through activity, the brain begins to reestablish balance, which is an important element in driving away depression. Walks, drives, initiating conversation, playing games, working on crafts, cooking—all of these activities form part of the plan for helping to lift depression.

"Some days you'll be unable to get your mother up and about, and you'll feel discouraged," I warned. "Many days we'll be unsuccessful in making activities happen for Elaine, but each day will be a new beginning with the schedule, and we may well succeed the next day."

I have encouraged this practice of getting up and getting out for many years. As one of my depressed residents started emerging from her emotional ditch, she said, "I feel bad, but I figure I'll feel bad, whether or not I do these activities. I may as well do a few of them; I may find I'll end up enjoying something."

Keeping active and following a schedule seldom make an immediate difference. At the beginning, depressed older people can look like zombies as they move through activities. But if we persist in keeping them up and going, the depression often starts to go away. And then some measure of enjoyment can return to life.

See If Medications Will Help

Treating depression with remembering and connecting and with getting the older person up and active is only part of the story. It always shocks me how much pain and depression go medically untreated among older people. It's as though our society thinks older people should have a certain amount of pain and depression, and it really isn't worth it to try to make things better.

Scripture doesn't teach that we sin when we seek the care of a doctor but rather that we are never to put our hope in a doctor over God. God is the ultimate physician, and doctors have only a limited ability to heal and help. But there is no heavenly rebuke for seeking help from a doctor for physical cure. Jesus himself said, "It is not the healthy who need a doctor, but the sick" (Matthew 9:12), and the apostle Paul calls Luke "the beloved physician" (Colossians 4:14 NKJV).

Elaine had been terribly undermedicated for her chronic pain. These days many new drugs can help long-standing problems, such as digestive tract issues and pain. A new class of pain medication helped Elaine enormously. I also suggested she be evaluated for treatment with an antidepressant.

I'm well aware of the dangers of overmedication and the risks of psychotropic drugs for the older brain. Yes, the use of antidepressant drugs comes with the risks of side effects. But almost all medications have such risks. For me, when allergy season comes around, I can either suffer with sinus problems, which eventually turn into infections, or I can take medication that will make my mouth dry and my body sleepy. I make the decision to take the allergy medication because the benefits of such medicine far outweigh the risks and the discomfort of not taking it. I believe the same is true with depression. Despite possible side effects, when a person is chemically imbalanced and suffers serious mental anguish, the potential benefits outweigh the risks.

Some people worry that taking antidepressants will "cover over" the real issue. We all have issues, and no pill will make them go away. Medications can bring a person to a mental state that allows him or her to constructively work on the issue. If you've ever seen a really depressed person—one who suffers from mental illness—then you know it makes clear thinking impossible. Are antidepressants the answer? Not completely, but certainly the new classes of medications, with minimal side effects, make sense in our day.

With that said, it's not easy to prescribe the right antidepressant for a person. No blood test or scan can tell a doctor what is the right medication to try. The doctor will prescribe a medication he or she *believes* will work effectively. Then the doctor will adjust dosages over the next several weeks and monitor improvement. If things don't get better, the doctor will prescribe another antidepressant. It often takes several months to find the right medication.

I sent Elaine to a geriatric psychiatrist who could evaluate her depression. He prescribed two psychotropic medications, and after three weeks she was showing steady improvement. Although the medication most likely was causing her to have some memory errors, her depression had been causing significant mental confusion, which was getting better.

I believe we have little excuse for failing to treat pain and depression in older people. We wouldn't be apathetic about seeking medical treatment for these issues in our children, and we shouldn't be apathetic about seeking treatment for our elders.

Encourage Ways to Resolve Old Issues

After a month, Elaine was showing marked improvement. We spent a little time each session remembering something from the past that helped her connect emotionally. Then we discussed applying that emotion in her everyday life. Her pain and chemical imbalance received proper treatment with medication, and she was responding well to that. But one issue represented a chronic problem.

At our seventh session, I asked Katie, "Tell me about how you know your mother cares about you and your children."

"Well," she responded, "she's always been kind to my kids. She's always been glad to see us, and we have nice visits."

"That's good," I replied, "but I get the feeling from Elaine and you that she spent most of her energy on your father and on her business and hasn't been much involved with you and your family."

Katie felt a bit threatened and retorted, "Mother and Daddy have been great parents, and they've never intentionally done anything to hurt any of us."

"I'm sure that's true," I said calmly, "but it isn't what I'm saying. Part of growing older is giving the younger generation emotional confidence and involvement so that they feel precious and important. It sounds as though Elaine has been a good parent but maybe hasn't been emotionally involved as you and your sister grew older."

Katie relaxed a little and said, "Yes, that's true. Mother and Daddy basically let us go when we left home. Some of that was good, but sometimes I wish they wouldn't have let go so much."

Elaine became very attentive as I spoke with Katie. "Tell me some of those things you wish your mother would have been more connected to in your family," I said.

Katie thought for a few moments and replied, "I don't know. Sometimes I wish we could sit and have a cup of coffee and discuss what's going on in my life instead of what's going on in hers. I really wish she'd be interested in having coffee with my two daughters and getting to know them and their lives better."

After exploring this awhile, I turned to Elaine and said, "You've done such a great job raising daughters, but it seems to me you might have become disconnected from them the last few years. Would you like to get some of that connection back?"

"I guess I *have* been too focused on myself," Elaine responded. "I do love all of them dearly."

"I can certainly sense how strongly you love them," I said. "I just think there's a way that an aging mom can reconnect to them to show how much you love them."

Elaine agreed, and I set up a schedule for her to go out to coffee with Katie or Katie's daughters once a week—at Elaine's expense—to find out what was going on with them.

After about three months, Elaine looked much better, and her depression had almost lifted. It wasn't one particular thing that made her better but a combination of helping her remember and connect, getting properly medicated, and responding as an emotional resource for her family. By the end of treatment, Elaine was going out with one of her daughters or grandchildren once a week to a favorite coffee shop. She spoke articulately and excitedly when she told me of all of the achievements of her children and grandchildren. Each time she came back to the personal care facility, she walked to the door, looked back at her family member, and said, "Be here later?"

THE SPIRITUAL LESSON OF DEPRESSION

What good is depression? If you've ever been depressed, you know the answer—"Nothing!" But, of course, it's the wrong question. The right question is, "What good can come from depression?" It's the question to focus on as we work through the muck and mire of this dark illness. It can be a difficult task to face, especially as Christians.

First, we struggle with the issue of whether depression is a sin. We hear the word *joy*, and we connect it with the fruit of the Spirit. Thus we reason that if we are in the Spirit, joy must be the result. If we are depressed, surely we must not be in the Spirit, and by definition we are entangled in sin.

Without question, an aspect of joy is the feeling of being overwhelmed with happiness and rejoicing. But another subtle meaning of joy can be found in the Bible, particularly in the New Testament—a form of joy based on *knowledge* and *hope*: "May the God of hope fill you with all joy and peace as you trust in him, so that you may overflow with hope by the power of the Holy Spirit" (Romans 15:13). The apostle Paul certainly knew struggles and pain. Although he often experienced happiness, he also endured intense suffering. And it was at these times that he most often wrote of his joy, based on the confidence that what God says is true and that the truth of Jesus' resurrection brings ultimate redemption. "That is why I am suffering as I am," Paul wrote. "Yet I am not ashamed, because I know whom I have believed, and am convinced that he is able to guard what I have entrusted to him for that day" (2 Timothy 1:12). This type of joy comes from the knowledge that God loves us and will stand by us and from the hope that we are fellow heirs to the benefits of the resurrection of Jesus.

Depression is no sin in and of itself; it is what we do with our depression that counts.

Several people whose stories are told in the Bible get depressed, but none strike me more than Job. Job endured repeated and devastating losses, suffered chronic pain, and without question suffered from mental depression. "God has made me a byword to everyone, a man in whose face people spit," he said. "My eyes have grown dim with grief; my whole frame is but a shadow" (Job 17:6–7). This well describes the curtain of depression that can hang overhead. And the responses of Job's wife and "friends" typify how many Christians still respond to depression.

- *Problem solve.* Job's friends seem more than eager to try to correct his spiritual deficiencies. Christians today do much the same when they try to talk someone out of his depression by attempting to "cheer him up." Trying to cheer up a depressed person is like trying to get someone who's in the middle of a chemotherapy regimen to compete in a decathlon. It simply cannot happen.

- *Blame God.* This insidious response basically reasons that, since God has done this evil to a depressed person, he or she should reject God. Job's wife clearly implores him to reject God: "Are you still holding on to your integrity? Curse God and die!" (Job 2:9). Some Christians do essentially the same thing to depressed people. If they don't respond to our efforts, we believe they lie beyond our help; thus we tend to drift away, to let them solve their problems alone. Essentially we say, "You're on your own. I don't know what to do with you, so I really don't even want to be around."

Modern society likes to give two related answers to depression: (1) get over it and feel joyful, or (2) reject the notion of a loving and good God, and therefore cut him out of your life. Of course, when you feel depressed this is exactly the temptation. You constantly ask yourself why you can't feel better, and you wonder if God has deserted you. It hurts to feel anything, even joy, because every feeling is awful.

In the midst of battling a deep depression of my own, I recall the gifted Henri Nouwen, pastor of the L'Arche Daybreak community until his death in 1996, saying to me, "Your depression may last the rest of your life. It came when you did not want it to come, and there is no promise that it will end. If the depression lasts the rest of your life, you must learn how to live your depression well."

Living depression well—it's the secret of how Job persisted through the depths of his despair. He couldn't escape his loss, social rejection, and physical ailments. Since there was no way he could get better on his own, he had to decide whether to reject God—for it seemed as though God had rejected him. But Job lived his depression well. He neither escaped the depression nor rejected God but instead held on to the *knowledge* and *hope* of God.

Depression takes us to the very edges of our existence. Although we may not sink to the depths Job experienced, it feels the same to us. When we get depressed, we look into an immense black hole where no feeling of hope exists and the knowledge of former happiness seems only an illusion. We are helpless to help ourselves and can't imagine ever feeling better. In our pain, we feel as though only two options exist—escape, or curse God. Either way, the answer feels like a sort of death.

But in the midst of this despair we discover the spiritual lesson. The answer is neither escape nor rejection but holding on to what we know about God. To live each day with the knowledge and hope that, even though things look, feel, and may actually be hopeless, we will still hold on to God.

If you've never been kissed by the precious agony of depression, you have no idea of what it feels like to fall off the edge of emotional stability. You don't know what it is to be in the midst of a fall to nowhere. You know nothing of having your senses blunted to the point where the air has a musty smell, food tastes bland, all touch hurts, and the color falls out of the world. But this place is no sin. Surely this place of depression does not represent what life is like without God.

Depression is a gift. It allows us to see the edge of ultimate despair and to have a choice: we cannot talk ourselves out of depression, and so we can either reject God because of the pain, or we can reach out to God despite the pain. The choice is clear and profound because depression forces us to the edge of the cliff, where we have nothing else to hold on to. In our desperation, when we reach out and hold on to God, we know we've passed a test that strengthens our faith. We know we've passed the same test Job faced. When we have nothing, and our whole lives have become shadows, we will hold on to the knowledge and hope of God.

This "holding on" doesn't necessarily make the depression lift; it helps us live our depression well. We, like Job, can say, "Naked I came from my mother's womb, and naked I will depart. The LORD gave and the LORD has taken away; may the name of the LORD be praised" (Job 1:21).

When we live depression well, we do what we can do. We practice emotional connection where we can, take care of ourselves physically to the best of our ability, and keep ourselves trying to do what we and the people around us know is right. We get up, we go to work, we speak with family members, and we fulfill our responsibilities. We live life—and our depression—well while we wait and see if God chooses to make our circumstances better. And if he does not, we hold on anyway.

COMMISSIONED TO A SPECIAL WORK

Although many caregivers will get depressed at one time or another, our elders are far more likely to experience deep depression. When I encounter an older person caught in a profound depression, I see myself in the role of Job's friends or wife. What will I say? Will I explore what he or she is doing wrong or what he or she should do to chase the depression away? Will I look at his or her life and agree that the situation stinks and that the time has come to pass on and die? Will I accuse God and question his promises, since he seems to have deserted this individual in pain?

In the worst of my own depression, several people stood by me and encouraged me to hold on. My wife, Sharon, was incredible as she helped hold me together. I also had a friend, Malcolm Street, who flew in to be with me from time to time. One day, when I was feeling particularly awful, he walked over and gave me a big hug. As he embraced me, he said, "I'll help you cry through this one."

As the older people we love sink into depression, God commissions us to a special work. No doubt we must help them remember and connect, get proper treatment, and resolve old issues. But the most important work we do will be in the reality of our presence and witness. We do what we can, but in the end we are witnesses to the older person's struggle to either reject or hold on to God. We cannot make the decision for them, but we can be witnesses to the joy born through the knowledge and hope of God. When heaviness and hopelessness reach their worst, we can hold them and help them cry through it.

QUESTIONS FOR CONSIDERATION

1. What do you believe about depression? Do you consider it to be a sin, or do you see it as an opportunity?

2. What do you believe about the medical treatment of depression? Where can you get additional information to become better educated about treatment?

3. What practical situations from the past could help an older person remember and connect emotionally?

10

We All Get
Stung by Death

The sting of death is sin, and the power of sin is the law.
1 Corinthians 15:56

Louis labored to breathe in his final hours of life. The members of his family who lived several hundred miles away had been called but hadn't yet arrived to say their good-byes. So I sat with Louis in the hospital room while he drifted in and out of consciousness.

At one point, his eyes opened wide, and a smile crept across his pale, haggard face. "Bonnie," he said, "it's so good to see you." (Bonnie was the name of his wife of forty-seven years, who had died almost five years before.) Unable to resist, I leaned forward and whispered, "Do you see Bonnie now?"

"Oh yes!" he replied. "I see everyone so clearly now."

Louis died within the hour.

Hallucination? Who am I to say? I certainly believe in a spiritual world beyond what I can see and touch, and although I know we join Jesus when we die, I'm far from sure of the logistics of that final journey. Still, I think it was quite possible that in his last moments Louis had more awareness of the spiritual world than he did of the physical. Perhaps he had entered that precarious "between" point where we make our transition from life on earth to everlasting life. He could answer me, but he seemed much more aware of his loved ones who had gone on before.

We Christians are even now in training for that "between" moment. We are citizens of a physical world, yet we're guaranteed citizenship in the heavenly kingdom. It can be a hard mix as we struggle to make sense of how to live in a place limited by time and space, with all our physical needs of food, water, and shelter. And yet we are guaranteed the innumerable, unfathomable riches of God through Jesus. Living in between our two worlds is messy work.

It's no wonder that, in an effort to try to solve the messiness, we often pretend as though it doesn't exist. We live as though God plays only a small part in our lives as we manage our affairs on our own, or we live in a la-la land where we pretend that God voids all our physical pains and heartaches. The messiness of the "between" tempts us to sell out to one side of the truth or the other.

As a result, we often live with half-truths. We may not have bad theology or inaccurate beliefs, but we prefer to concentrate only on the Bible verses that make us feel good about ourselves and God. Death, for example, sometimes prompts us to focus on a half-truth. We devour the comforting words at the funeral of a loved one: "Death has been swallowed up in victory. Where, O death, is your victory? Where, O death, is your sting?" (1 Corinthians 15:54–55). These words are wonderfully true because of the sacrifice of Jesus, who paid for the punishment of our sins through his death. This glorious fact assures us we will one day put on the imperishable clothing of immortality.

But the sting of death really *does* have a sting. The truth is, for however long God sees fit, we suffer with a perishable body that is doomed to die. Our justification, salvation, and sanctification as members of God's kingdom are a matter of record on God's timeline, but on our timeline we still exist as citizens of a fallen world. And so we live with the consequence: "By the sweat of your brow you will eat your food until you return to the ground, since from it you were taken; for dust you are and to dust you will return" (Genesis 3:19).

The full truth is that, while death has no *final* sting for us, nevertheless it stings us all. Because we have grown used to dealing with only half the truth about death, we often have difficulty dealing with and understanding death. We don't like to talk about it, acknowledge its implications on our relationships, or effectively deal with the problems it poses.

But the picture of aging forces us to look at death squarely in the eye. Being old means that death is not some vague possibility but, in fact, is just on the horizon and looming larger every day. To ignore death is to fail to acknowledge the elephant in the room. Nevertheless, many of us try to do just that, because ignoring death has become a social norm.

AVOIDANCE IS THE NORM

Sometime in the early twentieth century, the topic of death began to be put away—stuffed into the background of our social consciousness. As the nineteenth century had drawn to a close, a whole generation of Americans had lost family members in the Civil War. In addition, one could hardly find a clan that didn't have someone who had died in childbirth, from influenza or infection, or from an accident. Most families in the 1800s experienced death up close and very personally. Sick or injured family members received treatment primarily in the home, so most people had their final moments in the same bed where they had slept for years. Even the preparing of the body for burial and the viewing or "visitation" of the corpse occurred in the kitchen and parlor, respectively. In the nineteenth century, no one enjoyed death, but people were much better acquainted with dealing with the problems it presents than we are today.

As the twentieth century progressed, things changed radically. Medical science achieved great progress in the diagnosis and treatment of ailments, infections, and injuries. A massive push to build community hospitals took place, and more often than not, sick people returned from their hospital visits cured. So we drifted into thinking that no problem was so great that skilled hospital doctors could not fix it. People started going to the hospital for any serious sickness—and they also began to die there.

Today, almost 86 percent of us will die in some type of medical facility, and, for the most part, we'll be dying in isolation from the people who love us the most. When death occurs, we much prefer to take our dead to the funeral "home" to prepare and bury the corpse rather than deal with the gruesome reality ourselves. (Note how we've even stopped using "parlor" to describe a room in our home because it evoked the image of "funeral parlor"; we now refer to the front entertainment area as a "living room.")

Although death has been effectively removed from our everyday thinking, as caregivers we cannot avoid its implications. Like everything God has put in our lives, death has something deep and important to teach us. But in order to understand what death has to teach us about life, we have to once again *embrace* the end instead of shoving it to the back of our consciousness.

STOP THE AVOIDANCE

I'm not suggesting we start placing our dead relatives on our dining room tables to prepare their bodies for burial. I would recommend, however, that we pull a little closer to death without fear or avoidance.

Eighty-eight-year-old Eddie was moving from one serious health issue to the next. A longtime smoker, Eddie had had part of a lung removed, suffered from congestive heart failure, and was on the verge of kidney failure. At the time of Eddie's hospitalization, he weighed 135 pounds; he now weighed a mere 105. He drifted in and out of consciousness, sometimes not recognizing his two adult children, Mason and Madison.

I truly believe a five-year-old could have known Eddie was dying. I knew it; the doctors certainly knew it. But for some reason, Eddie and his children weren't able to acknowledge it. In his conscious moments, Eddie mumbled about leaving the hospital. Mason insisted that doctors keep treating his father's various ailments.

Eddie did die after two full months of treatment. He lay in a coma for the last fifteen days of his life, exhausting all of his resources. Still, Mason vehemently accused the doctors of malpractice. It was a very sad ending to a very sorry circumstance.

What I'm about to say is controversial—and I don't say it lightly. While the Bible clearly tells us that killing another person is a sin, it also clearly points out the inevitability of death for all of us:

> Just as man is destined to die once, and after that to face judgment, so Christ was sacrificed once to take away the sins of many people; and he will appear a second time, not to bear sin, but to bring salvation to those who are waiting for him.
>
> Hebrews 9:27–28

Many of us have become guilty of a sin that's the opposite of murder. We have tried to keep people from their appointed time of death.

I'm not speaking of physician-assisted suicide, in which a terminally ill person makes the choice to end his or her life, under the supervision of a doctor, before the end comes naturally. I believe taking one's life is wrong, for the same reasons

I believe murder is wrong. But I also find little justification for dramatic and expensive treatments when the older person is clearly headed toward death. Certainly we can find justifications for heroic medical treatment aimed at saving a young or middle-aged person who has years of development in front of him or her. But part of being old is the reality that our development is complete, and, like it or not, our stories have largely been written.

An eighty-eight-year-old person who is in the same condition as Eddie will die. He or she can die today or tomorrow or, with profound medical effort, in two months. But he or she *will* die, and there will be no significant change in his or her life story. It's truly tragic when a young person in the prime of life dies without completing the normal life sequence, but I believe it's also tragic to use extraordinary medical efforts to keep a person alive when he or she has reached his or her time to die.

We treat older people much too long for many different reasons, including our expectation that we can treat and overcome *any* physical threat. Medical science has simply outrun the ethics required to determine its good use. A person in the advanced stage of Alzheimer's eventually will die. If he or she contracted pneumonia, is it proper to administer antibiotic treatment to prolong life? It's a difficult question, but I'll step out on a limb and say, "No, I don't think so." When I make this statement in public, I'm often called names and labeled a person who endorses euthanasia. I counter, once again, that when a person's life story has been written and his development finished, while we don't have the right to take away his life, neither do we have the right to resist death on his behalf.

I have the highest regard for the sanctity of life, but I also have a high regard for death. We're *destined to die once, and after that to face judgment.* It is a scary thing to die—and scarier still to face judgment. At the heart of it, I believe we sometimes try to improperly extend an older person's life because we fear death and judgment. We are afraid of it for ourselves, and we are afraid of it for someone else.

Please don't misunderstand. I'm not suggesting that we withhold food from an older person or that there is no value in caring for an older person who is approaching death. I am saying that we have no right to play God with regard to when a living person should die, nor do we have any right to play God with regard to declaring when a dying person should live. Modern medicine has made it more and more possible to achieve the latter, and it's time for Christians to take a good, long, hard look at the full truth of the issue.

Instead of investing so much in the medical treatment of an older person who is close to death, I believe we should invest our time in helping the older person *die well*. Only then can we stop our avoidance of death and approach the meaning and process God intended to communicate when he introduced death to the human race. Our older parent cannot teach us how to avoid death, but he or she *can* teach us to die well.

James Madison, the father of the United States constitution, was an older man—his political career long over—when he said, "Having outlived so many of my contemporaries, I ought not to forget that I may be thought of to have outlived myself." In our society of advanced medical technology, it's a very real possibility that many of us will outlive ourselves. When we have reached our last stage of development—true old age— and when our lives' stories lie behind us, we need to be willing to fall into the hands of God, and we must be willing to let our older parents do the same.

MAKING DYING A VICTORY

When Napoleon conquered Europe, he set his sights on overrunning the vast expanse of Russia. Nothing looked more desperate than the plight of the Russians, ill equipped to wage war against the most powerful and best-trained army in the world. Straight to Moscow Napoleon marched his army, with very little resistance.

When he arrived in Moscow, however, he discovered much of the city in ruins, burned by the Russians themselves. In the dead of winter and with few supplies left, Napoleon had no choice but to withdraw his troops on a long retreat to France. Precisely at this time the Russians attacked and pursued his army into almost total annihilation. Napoleon had made it to Moscow triumphantly, but in his "victory" he set the stage for his ultimate defeat and the rebirth of Russia.

Satan no doubt considered the prospect of Jesus' death one of the ultimate victories of his reign of terror. With Jesus dead and buried, he must have gloated and celebrated over the accomplishment of his fondest goal. But Jesus had become human "so that by his death he might destroy him who holds the power of death—that is, the devil—and free those who all their lives were held in slavery by their fear of death" (Hebrews 2:14–15). In the end, Jesus overcame death with his resurrection. Like Napoleon, Satan's "victory" served only to set the table for a most bitter meal of defeat. Jesus' resurrection put the coup de grâce to Satan's reign and will one day result in the devil's being cast into eternal darkness. What so clearly looked like defeat for Jesus actually set the stage for his ultimate victory.

Death cannot quench our hope if we will persist in waiting for the promised resurrection of humankind. In the meantime, we have the promise of time as one generation conceives, gives birth to, and nurtures to maturity the next generation. As each generation lives, dies, and passes on, it reminds us that time serves to display the history of God's faithfulness in bringing forth the kingdom of God. In the death of the oldest generation, we remember the defeat of death;

but in the next generation that lives on, we also recall the hope of the resurrection.

One reason I love working with aging families is that so much of what is truly important in the family comes down to the intergenerational exchange. It is like a relay race where the older parent comes around the final stretch to hand off the baton to you. In the exchange, there is a great opportunity to deal with old, unresolved issues, and chart out what the elder has learned from his or her long trek around the track of life.

TALKING ABOUT DEATH AND MAKING PLANS

"I'm uncomfortable talking about the end," Jeanette said, "even though I think we both know it's near." Jeanette had heard me talk at a community meeting about the topic of grief and wanted to come in to see me with her mother. Jeanette's mother, "Babs," had colon cancer, and at the age of seventy-five, she was entering her last few weeks of life. "I think we have things we should talk about, but I just don't know how to get to them," Jeanette confessed.

Once you move from trying so hard to keep your aging parent alive to preparing for death, expect a certain amount of discomfort. Like Jeanette, most of us feel the need to deal with the issue with our parent. It would be nice if our older parent would bring up the subject, but it rarely happens. If the subject of death is going to be broached, the caregiver is usually the one who has to do it.

I usually suggest that the caregiver begin by talking about the issues the older parent has already been facing concerning death. After getting to know Jeanette and Babs, I looked at Babs and said, "You've lived much longer than I, so I would imagine you've outlived many of those you've been closest to."

"Yes," Babs said, "I buried my husband about twenty years ago. He died from a heart attack."

"Do you have siblings and parents?" I asked.

"I have an older sister who is still alive and in good health," she replied, "but, of course, my parents died many years ago. My mother died of cancer."

"Did your mother die suddenly?" I asked.

"No," she answered, "she lived for about a year after she underwent surgery, and she was in bad shape for about the last two months."

When I saw Jeanette's face register surprise at hearing this, I asked her, "Did you know about your grandmother's cancer?"

"I knew she died of cancer," Jeanette replied, "but I never really knew she had lingered."

Almost always, the older parent has past experiences with death that will open up an opportunity to direct the conversation toward the present circumstance. I looked at Babs and asked, "Before your mom died, were you able to speak with her about her wishes, or did she leave it for the family to sort out?"

"We really were left on our own," Babs said. "I always regretted not talking to my mom more in those last few months."

"It's a difficult thing to talk about death," I observed. "It's uncomfortable because we don't want to offend anyone. But some things are so important I find that we must talk about them or we'll live with regret. Have you two been able to talk about the possibility of death?" Both Jeanette and Babs looked at one another and then answered no. This gave us the opportunity to move toward talking about Babs's impending death.

I always try to talk first about the logistics of death—the wishes of each family member with regard to the funeral and the deceased's belongings. We discuss a wide range of subjects, most of which fit into three main categories—finances, beliefs, and funeral details. I've already talked about some of the ins and outs of the legal and financial picture of elders (see chapter 7), but an impending death provides an excellent time to make sure these details get fully planned.

I think it's important to find out what the older parent believes about death. Many older parents and caregivers have never spoken openly about spiritual subjects. Death forces us to consider these beliefs more directly. I usually let both the older parent and caregiver express their ideas about God, mortality, and heaven. Sometimes these issues take several sessions, and often it results in either the older parent or caregiver sharing the gospel with the other. These powerful moments can change the life direction of an entire generation.

Both Jeanette and Babs had a strong Baptist background, but neither had ever discussed openly their beliefs about heaven. In the third session, Babs said to Jeanette, "I know I'm a believer and I will be with Jesus. I'll see you on the other side, and I'll be waiting for you when your time comes."

Jeanette embraced her mother and said, "I know. We'll hug just like this."

Funerals represent a significant issue that families must meet head-on. The ritual of burial has been performed from the beginning of human history. The community comes together to mark the beliefs, transitions, and recognitions that occur at death. The philosophy of a funeral is a personal thing, but I usually observe that family members either want to use the occasion to honor the life of the older parent or to comfort mourners. I believe good funerals do both.

"I guess I don't want a funeral that's just sad," Babs said. "I want people to know I'm in a better place. I want them to know I'll be waiting to give them a hug when they get there."

Jeanette and her mother discussed many details. Together they chose a funeral director and purchased a casket. They picked out hymns and met with Babs's minister so he could hear about the things they wanted said about her at the funeral. Babs even wrote out a little poem to be given to mourners. Jeanette told me at the end of the fifth session, "Talking about Mom's death is so freeing. I never dreamed she would take the lead once we opened the subject up. I'm sad about losing my mother, but this process makes it so much easier."

MAKING SENSE OUT OF LIFE: THE EXCHANGE OF WISDOM

While a person's life and story are precious, the words of the story usually get blended into one long, run-on paragraph. We usually wait for a eulogy to try to make some sense out of the older person's life. But I believe it's the job of every older parent and caregiver to help make sense of the elder's story before he or she dies.

By articulating the important stories, gleaning the wisdom learned, and remembering the accomplishments, the long paragraph gets punctuated with all the commas, periods, and section breaks that clarify the intended meaning. After an older person gets comfortable discussing the topic of death, it's good to pursue the meaning of his or her life through story.

Sometimes the story of a person's life flows very easily, but in the instances where it becomes difficult, I usually try to help by thinking in terms of the developmental periods of life. It is reasonable to divide life into early childhood (0 to 12 years), adolescence (13 to 20 years), young adulthood (20 to 40 years), middle adulthood (40 to 60 years), and late adulthood. It can be useful to help the older parent organize meaning around these time periods.

"I learned from my family that you always stay loyal to one another" goes one statement of meaning surrounding childhood. If I were to hear such a statement from an older person, I'd seek a story from his or her family background that shows how this belief came to be learned. In these stories we find the real meaning and wisdom of a person's life.

Although Babs now felt comfortable talking about death, she had trouble conceptualizing things about her past. It can be helpful to start the conversation by relating historical events to the developmental periods of the older person's life. For example, Babs was born in the late 1920s, and so the Great Depression took place during her childhood and she reached adolescence during World War II. When I refer to what I know about these historical events, it can spur the older person to relate specific stories that help to clarify life. When I mentioned World War II, Babs told of her father serving in the Navy in the Pacific Theater. Her mother moved her and her sister to the West Coast to take a job in a factory. For the most part, Jeanette had never heard the story.

"Those were some memorable times," Babs said, "but I really learned how important freedom was to us. My dad served in the Navy, but I felt like all of us were serving the war effort." The story allowed the content of Babs's beliefs to come forth and her wisdom to be expressed.

Many people videotape or audiotape these stories. In this day of technology, it's very easy to edit and transfer these conversations into meaningful programs that capture the essence of the older person. I have a lovely story of how my grandmother and grandfather moved to northern New Mexico after they married—complete with photographs and period music. The capturing of the story and then editing it into a program takes time, but it becomes a precious gift of wisdom to future generations.

Some older people, however, do not have happy stories or stories that seem to have produced much wisdom. Some have stories of tragedies, and some, sadly, have stories of wasted lives. I still believe it's important to hear about these hard times and failures, because these stories also do carry a message of wisdom. Relaying and reviewing the past helps the older person work out unresolved issues while helping future generations avoid mistakes and keep from wasting the precious gift of life.

THE GIVING OF A BLESSING

The Old Testament book of Genesis relates several stories of the generational torch being passed. When the older person is ready to pass on and the offspring is poised to fill the place, this is the time when the elder gives a blessing. Blessings, like funerals, serve more as a ritual of passage than anything else. For instance, when Jacob blessed Joseph, Joseph had already become a man of God:

> Joseph is a fruitful vine,
>> a fruitful vine near a spring,
>> whose branches climb over a wall.
> With bitterness archers attacked him;
>> they shot at him with hostility.
> But his bow remained steady,
>> his strong arms stayed limber,
> because of the hand of the Mighty One of Jacob,
>> because of the Shepherd, the Rock of Israel.
>> Genesis 49:22–24

The blessing of Jacob did nothing for Joseph that hadn't already been done. Blessing does, however, make a tremendous difference to both the older parent and the child. It gives the older parent an opportunity to recognize what and who his or her offspring has become. When we view our offspring through the lens of blessing them, we state the truth of how God has used us to shape their personhoods. It gives the older person the chance to know that the lineage of the family is left in good hands. The blessing fills the child who receives it with the confidence necessary to lead and to carry on. To hear a parental blessing is like hearing, "You really are something. Take your place as a full-fledged adult. I have confidence in you, and I'm proud of you." Whether you are sixteen or sixty-five, you will never cease to be moved by this type of pronouncement.

We are generally not a society of ritual, so I like to help older parents get an idea of what they'd like to say about themselves and their offspring. For the older parent, I ask questions like, "What would you like people to say about you when you're gone?" or "What would you like as an epitaph on your gravestone?" I also help them conceptualize the blessing to give to a child by asking something like, "If you had one opportunity to say one last thing to your child, what would it be?"

Toward the end of Babs's eighth and final session, she had become noticeably weak. We talked quite a bit about the last words she wanted to leave with her children, but she didn't want to say them in the session. About two weeks after Babs's death, I received a note from Jeanette:

> I wanted to let you know that when Mom knew her death was very near, she called me to her bed for "something important." She said, "You have always been my hero. You have always been my daughter. I know that God is proud of you. I will be waiting for you when it is your time."

CAREGIVING FOR A DYING PARENT

Very few of our older parents will "slip away" in their sleep during the night. If we're doing the job of caregiving, it's likely our older parent has been chronically ill and on a slow decline for quite some time. As a result, the process of dying is often long and drawn out.

I consider the hospice movement to be one of the real blessings of our day. When doctors can prescribe no further treatment for a dying person, they often refer the family and individual to a hospice—which is essentially a philosophy instead of an organization. Some chapters operate out of local hospitals, while others are run by for-profit organizations. For the most part, hospices around the world are committed to providing a safe, loving, supportive environment for individuals and families in which their loved ones can die with dignity and respect. Hospice care is typically covered by Medicare.

When you believe your older parent has deteriorated to the point of near death, I urge you to speak with the doctor not only about treatment options but also about death options. When the caregiver brings up this issue, it often gives the doctor permission to speak freely concerning the older parent's prognosis. If the doctor doesn't believe death is near, usually he or she won't hesitate to say so and then explain the circumstances that would indicate when the time has come. Most often, though, when the caregiver senses that death is near, it usually is. This allows the doctor to speak about options for making the older parent's death as dignified and pain free as possible.

As the caregiver, don't hesitate to talk with the doctor about the wishes expressed by you and your parent. It's usually best for the older person to stay in his or her home environment as long as possible, so your goal can be to try to bring support to the home instead of taking the older parent to support outside of the home environment. Comfort, love, and blessings are much more likely to be spoken in the context of a familiar environment than in a hospital. Doctors and hospices as a rule support this desire. They will seek to manage your parent's pain so he or she can remain as alert and engaged as possible during the final weeks, days, or hours.

If it becomes necessary for your parent to be hospitalized, a hospice often has special facilities and rooms that feel aesthetically pleasing and comfortable for the family. But whether in the home, hospital, or hospice facility, the hospice will pay particular attention to your older parent and your family as you deal with the grief of the impending death.

Can you go it alone? Yes. Realize, however, that the process of dying can be grueling and very painful for the older person. Many times I've seen a caregiver who was committed to being the only one to care for his or her parent go through weeks of care with only minimal rest. This caregiver can finally reach a point of exhaustion and must care for himself or herself just as the older parent dies.

No support is perfect, but I believe hospice services will most often provide the necessary support so you can continue to do your job as caregiver until the very end.

AT THE MOMENT OF DEATH

Several years ago I spoke to a doctor who had no belief in God. When I asked, "When it comes time for you to die, what do you want to happen at the end?"

"I just want someone I love and who loves me to hold my hand," he said.

It is a privilege to be present when our parent dies. It is the opportunity to hold his or her hand and give it one last squeeze before we pass our loved one into the hands of God.

At the moment of death, however, there is more to our job than simple presence. Our job also consists of *permission*. Many times, older people sense that we're not ready to let them go or that we may be feeling overwhelming pain. It seems to happen quite often that caregivers will go home to get some rest or step out for a bite to eat, and then receive notification that their parents have died. It seems clear to me that the older parent waited to die until he or she was alone, so as to ease the immediate pain of the caregiver. I've seen this phenomenon both when the older parent is conscious and also when he or she is unconscious. The older person's ability to sense the emotional context around him or her seems profound.

I often suggest that it's helpful to give the older parent permission to die. I'll never forget the time a daughter was hovering over the bed of her unconscious mother, who was laboring with each breath. The daughter tenderly took the mother's hand and said, "Mother, I love you very much and will miss you, but it's OK to let go. We will be all right, and you don't need to struggle anymore." She kissed her mother's forehead, and the mother heaved a heavy sigh and then breathed her last. Since witnessing this, I've often recommended that families give the older parent permission to let go. I have found it can be a comforting release for the parent and can get the grief work of the family off to a good start.

THE SPIRITUAL LESSON OF DYING

We often hear the cliché "Death is just part of life." While there is some truth to the statement, it is oxymoronic at best.

Death, in many ways, is death—plain and simple. The judgment we face in death is the judgment that sin has overcome our ability to live. It is the final decaying answer to our wish to achieve immortality without God. If you've ever touched a dead body, you know just how hopeless that wish is.

Such was the scene when Jesus arrived too late to heal his friend Lazarus. Lazarus had died four days before Jesus' arrival. When Jesus instructed the family to remove the stone from the entrance to Lazarus's tomb, they were worried that the smell of rotting flesh would be overpowering. But Jesus persisted, and after he prayed, he said, "Lazarus, come out!" (John 11:43). Lazarus came out, not in resurrection, but in *resuscitation.*

We have no hope of staving off death; we do not look for resuscitation. We hope that Jesus will call us out from the grave into true resurrection, complete with a new body—the kind that can never perish and is fit for the heavenly kingdom. It's the kind of body like the one Jesus had after his own resurrection—a body that could eat, be touched, and carry on conversations, yet was clearly and dramatically different from what it was before. In order to take part in this resurrection, however, we have to relinquish our desire for resuscitation. We must, in a word, die—finally and for good.

This is the risk we face in the dying and death of our older parents. It's also the risk we face ourselves. We must face the reality that all of our caregiving ultimately ends in futility. Our parent ends up the very same way every human being has ended up since the inception of the planet—he or she will die. And we must let them fall into that place of defeat, into the hands of a loving but also scary God.

Depression teaches us that we ultimately can do nothing and that we must hang on to God. Death teaches us that we can hang on to nothing; all we can do is let go. We do not know, at least in detail, what happens to us. We do not know how we will be transformed. We do not even know if we will know that it is happening. All we know is that we will be forced to let go and totally trust in God and in his power to provide for us and resurrect us.

This is the lesson of dying. It's the final letting go amidst our undeniable defeat. It is letting God have his way when we can do nothing else. And we have the promise that when we so surrender, we will partake in resurrection.

It's Hard to Lose a Hero

Almost all of us have heroes. One of mine was Rick Husband. He and his wife, Evelyn, participated in a summer Bible study program Sharon and I sponsored during the late 1970s. We kept in touch through the years and felt thrilled when Rick fulfilled his lifelong dream of becoming a NASA astronaut. We felt privileged, not only that Rick and Evelyn shared their lives with us, but also that they shared the thrill of space with our children.

Rick commanded the STS-107 crew of the space shuttle Columbia. Everyone knows about that particular shuttle mission. It blazed an image into our consciousness forever when it disintegrated over the skies of Texas. It was a tragedy to see such a good Christian man lost. It hurt terribly to see Evelyn and her children suffer from the loss. Our community, and rightly so, gathered several times to honor Rick's memory through services, dedications, and monuments. Evelyn has faithfully shared in a public forum how God's mercy and faithfulness can sustain—even in the hardest of times.

It is a hard thing to lose a hero.

But selfishly, what about us? No one is going to rush out and name an airport in our older parent's honor. No one will remember our love and sacrifice in providing care, cleaning up filthy messes, serving the most basic of functions. No one will remember our pain. There will be no monument.

There are few heroes in aging. There's not much that's glamorous about it, and no one wants to live vicariously through our experiences. We are, in many ways, alone—like a tree that falls, unwitnessed, in the woods. It may make a sound, but *no one hears* its heavy crashing.

At least, not here.

Our hope does not lie in the greatness of the feat but in the faithfulness of the act. This happens in two ways:

- The Creator takes notice that when we care for the sick, infirm, and incompetent, we do so as unto Christ (Matthew 25:40). This is no small thing. It means we're actually present in his pain and sufferings. And just at the crucial moments of Christ's need, we are there to do the ministering—helping with the cross, wiping his brow, giving a drink of water, and clothing him. When we reach out and do these things to the one in need, we participate in the privilege of serving Christ.

- We leave a legacy for those around us—and it's not because our families remember our names or because our tombstones will say, "They cared well for their aging parents." Long after we're gone, our work of trustworthy care will remain written on the hearts of our children. True love always willingly reaches out to put another's needs ahead of its own. Our trustworthy action will get translated into a transcendent truth that will stand as a legacy of strength for our children to follow—perhaps when it is our time to age.

Trustworthy action gets translated in a thousand ways. Even now, as we head toward the finish line of aging and caregiving with Genevieve, we actively exchange both trust and love. When my children play the piano for Genevieve, and she joyfully claps her hands on her knees in excitement. When Sharon cuts her mother's food into smaller and smaller pieces and massages her cheeks to remind her to swallow. When having her grandson introduced to her for the hundredth time brings the response, "He's good-looking." When she describes the "big trees" over and over again while riding in the car, and we patiently listen to her attempts at conversation. When Sharon, our son, and our daughter hug Genevieve in succession and say, "I love you," even when she cannot respond. When I hold out my hand to take her to the bathroom, and she automatically reaches out in trust to find my palm.

When we come to the end of life, we discover that "loving your parents when they can no longer love you" is a misnomer. The truth is, it's not our parents' fault that they can no longer love us; it is age itself that robs them of the physical strength, the mental acumen, and the energy to give more.

We face the same reality. We love, not in our own strength, but within the rhythm of life that God has set up—just as once it was our parents' moment to love within their own rhythm of time. They *do* love us, but everything about their body is heading toward death. We love them, knowing they'll die anyway and our efforts will, in many ways, go down the drain.

We don't love because it does any earthly good. Remember Jesus' commands to care for the poor and the prisoners—but also remember that he insists the poor will always be with us. We cannot *solve* the problems of aging with love, any more than we can solve poverty with love. Yet we are commanded to love. Why? Because it changes our lives. It gives us some sense of healing. It "fixes" us, not out of our strength, but out of our weaknesses. Love points out where we need to be healed.

When it comes to our elders, love gives us someone to lament. Love causes us to say good-bye, to hold their hands as they grab hold of the Lord. For us, love gives the privilege of seeing the passage and prepares us for our own journey, just as it models for the coming generations how to give without any hope of getting repaid. This is how we learn what it is like to be like Christ.

Giving out of our own deficit to that which appears to be the most decayed—this is what loving our elders is like in the face of death. It appears to be the furthest thing from life and hope. Surely this is what we must look like to Christ when he continues to give his full measure to us.

Of course, we are not God, and we struggle to love, even as we try to put on our best faces. But through God's grace and communion with Jesus Christ, we can love yet one more day. If we are truly tender, then God can infiltrate even that unloving part of our character and remake us at the core of who we are—changing our hearts for the long run. And when we are changed through the task of giving care, then hope is born for others in our family line to change. Future generations can be changed until we all meet at the resurrection. And when that day comes, our older parent will be there waiting for us—to love us once again.

QUESTIONS FOR CONSIDERATION

1. What thoughts do you have about the kind of medical care that may be utilized to keep your parent alive?

2. How will you know when it's your parent's time to die?

3. How can you help your parent constructively talk about death and the meaning of his or her life, and how can you ask for a final blessing?

We want to hear from you. Please send your comments about this book to us in care of zreview@zondervan.com. Thank you.

ZONDERVAN™

GRAND RAPIDS, MICHIGAN 49530 USA

WWW.ZONDERVAN.COM